Claws in the Air

A true-life adventure
thundering through the sky in the
Barrier Reef Airways flying boat
VH-BRA *Beachcomber*
bound for Heron Island.

The sky darkens. There is a
rumble of thunder…

FOR
KLAUS
wherever
he may
be

ANTHONY BARTON

Claws in the Air

Passengers are being ferried out to the *Beachcomber* in
a launch. One can just make out, on the tail, the
emblem of Barrier Reef Airways.

Bulmer Press

Claws in the Air

Bulmer Press Edition

Library and Archives Canada Cataloguing in Publication
Barton, Anthony, 1942-, author Claws in the air/Anthony
Barton (Books about Claws; 2)
ISBN 978-1-927721-23-0 (paperback)
1. Barton, Anthony, 1942 - -- Childhood and youth. 2.
Aeronautics—Flights. 3. Authors, Canadian (English) –
21st Century – Biography. I. Title
PS8553.A7776Z53 2016 C813'.6 C2016-900095-8

Books by Anthony Barton

Novels
Claws in the Air
The Revenge of Claws
Teresa

The Harriman Adventures
Midshipman Harriman
Lieutenant Harriman
Captain Harriman

Books for Children
Bat Rider
The Yumi Trees
The Bat Riders of Yumi

Comic Books
Rainbow Jane's Comic Book 1
Rainbow Jane's Comic Book 2
Rainbow Jane's Comic Book 3

Non-Fiction
Life and Breath
On the Methods of Famous Teachers
On the Structure of Didactic Tales

1: The Bus to Colmslie

I STOOD with my parents in Adelaide Street outside the Tourist Bureau on a cold, windy morning waiting for the bus to take us to the flying boat at Colmslie. It was confused. I had arrived in Oz and everything was upside down. The seasons had been reversed. I blamed this on the Winged Monkeys.

When the bus came it was a Comet with a four-foot high streamlined grill and protruding fender headlamps, painted maroon and cream, with whitewall tires and chrome details.

'Wizzo!' I said.

Dad swung me up the steps, and then I turned to help Mum because she had put on weight during our five-week voyage to Melbourne. Dad was an officer in the navy.

The great thing about being a child is that you may count on your parents to arrange interesting things for you to do. Here we were taking this trip out to Heron Island on the Great Barrier Reef. We were off to catch a plane. I was excited. Not for one moment did I suspect that I would find myself at the controls of that plane, or that things were going to go seriously wrong.

I had no idea I was heading into danger.

Mum took up two whole seats on the bus.

I sat with Dad.

The bus driver shifted gears. We growled out onto the road. As we picked up speed I decided it was time for a little light conversation.

'Did you ever kill anyone in the war?' I asked my father.

He raised one eyebrow and regarded me thoughtfully. 'Not personally,' he replied. 'But indirectly I must have been responsible for the deaths of many.'

I liked Dad. He took my questions seriously.

I decided to cheer him up.

'Never mind,' I said. 'Tell me a story.'

Dad's stories were crackers.

He made up his tales as he went along.

He was a hopeless storyteller.

His characters did not even have proper names.

So I had to help.

That was part of the fun.

Dad stuck his tongue into his cheek, narrowed his eyes, and looked at me sideways.

This was the best bit. Watching his face.

You could *see* him trying to think up a plot.

Dad was the opposite of Mum.

Mum recited ding-dong poems she had learned by heart at school, and taught me to *hear* words, while Dad taught me to *fashion* them.

I would live with my parents forever. There would be just the three of us. I was nine, and altruism was a long word.

We bumped along in the Comet bus.

The characters in my father's stories were fishes. They were always the *same* three fishes.

'So?' I said, trying out the bus seat to see how bouncy it was. 'What are Sponge, X and Y up to today?'

I knew how his story would begin.

All of his stories began the same way: *Sponge, X and Y were swimming along in the sea.*

Dad was such a klutz.

His three fishes were called Sponge, X and Y because he could think of no better names for them. He wasn't much good at thinking up plots, either. He always began *in medias res*. His three fishes would be swimming along and then they would meet an octopus, or they would find an old boot lying on the sea floor.

This time they bumped into a Giant Clam. I was not sure what a Giant Clam was, but I hoped it was dangerous.

'The Giant Clam had its mouth open,' said Dad, and paused to look down at me.

I told you he was clueless.

I had to think fast to keep Dad's tale going.

I promoted Sponge to Lieutenant.

'Follow me!' cried Lieutenant Sponge of the Royal Fish Navy and swam bravely into the mouth of the Giant Clam!

Dad's jaw dropped.

My brilliant advance of the plot had left him gasping! Or was he laughing? It was hard to tell.

I pressed on eagerly.

The big fish X and the little brainy fish Y obeyed Sponge's order. They swam inside the Giant Clam. All three fishes were in danger!

I bit my thumb. I was a little ahead of myself. I wasn't sure *why* the three fishes were in danger.

I just wanted the story to be thrilling.

So Dad came to my rescue.

'Snap!' he said. 'The Giant Clam closed its mouth. The three fishes were trapped inside. It was dark inside the Giant Clam.'

The three fishes were trapped.

My eyes grew round and anxious. I was not at all sure my father would be able to think of a way for the three fishes to escape before the bus arrived and it was time to board our plane.

Dad looked at me helplessly.

He was stuck. His story was going nowhere, as usual. It was up to me.

I rapped on his bus seat. Dad regarded me gravely. He said: 'Y swam as fast he could and banged the inside of the Giant Clam with his nose. This made no difference. The Giant Clam did not hear him.'

I grew pale with worry. The Clam would have to receive some more obvious signal.

I rapped on the bus seat *three times*.

'He banged three times,' said my father.

My face lit up. Three times should do the trick!

'But still the Giant Clam paid no attention,' my father ploughed on.

I rolled my eyes.

Oh, Dad!

We would soon be boarding the plane. Not only was my father hopeless at telling stories; he was clueless when it came to ending them.

I clenched my fists. The story would be left incomplete.

I was beside myself with anxiety.

'Along came a fourth fish,' said Dad.

This time it was *my* jaw that dropped.

I was astounded. There had never before in *any* of Dad's stories been a *fourth* fish.

'The fourth fish was called M,' he went on.

'M?' I said, doubtfully. What sort of a stupid name was that for a fish?

'What's M like?' I asked anxiously.

'M is a linguist.'

'What's that?'

'Someone who speaks different languages.'

'Where did M learn to speak different languages?'

'She went to language school.'

'She speaks English?'

'Yes.'

'She speaks French?'

'Yes.'

'She speaks… Chinese?'

'Yes.'

'Wow! Not bad for a fish.'

'Shall I go on with the story?'

'Yes, please.'

Dad cleared his throat.

'M speaks the language of the Giant Clams,' he said.

I challenged my father: 'What does that language sound like?'

'Burp blop beep bap boop,' said Dad without hesitation.

I burst out laughing. 'Right,' I said.

'The Giant Clam understood at once what M was saying, and opened its mouth. Sponge, X and Y swam out into the open sea.'

'To meet M?' I asked, astonished.

'All three fishes rubbed noses with M to say thank you.'

I sighed with relief. Dad's story had ended in time. The bus had pulled up with a squeal of brakes. We were at Colmslie.

We helped Mum down the steps and into the launch. Together with other passengers we were ferried out to the Barrier Reef Airways Catalina flying boat VH-BRA *Beachcomber* bound for Heron Island. As the launch cleared the jetty, I saw the *Beachcomber* for the first time. She was a strange looking machine: a *floating plane* with two monstrous variable pitch propellers. I knew from *The Modern Boy's Book of Aircraft* that they were driven by Pratt & Whitney reciprocating engines.

The plane had one long thick airfoil deep camber wing braced with compression struts. Flaps located on the trailing edge of the wings were of the Fowler design giving better takeoff performance, permitting steeper approach angles, and lower approach and landing speeds.

While boarding the launch to go out to the plane, I had been joined by two people of my own age: my friend Annie and my enemy Claws.

They were to share the holiday with me.

A part of me would rather have had my parents all to myself, but another part of me was pleased to have company.

I was especially pleased to see Annie.

Annie's mother was an actress.

'Track in on seaplane,' said Annie.

'It's not a seaplane. It's a flying boat.'

'Track in on flying boat,' said Annie, undeterred. 'Drumroll. Spooky music. You look at me and say 'No worries, Annie. It's perfectly safe.'

'No worries, Annie. It's perfectly safe.'

'Good,' said Annie. 'Now the audience knows we're in terrible danger.'

'They do?' I was surprised. I understood that the audience was imaginary, but still...

Claws regarded the *Beachcomber* with growing alarm. 'Vere is der undercarriage?' he demanded. Claws was our nemesis.

'There is no undercarriage, Claws,' I said. 'The plane floats on the water. That's why they call it a flying boat.'

Claws looked up at the sky. 'Bad weather come.'

'You're barmy, Claws,' I said.

I spotted the *Beachcomber*'s portside gun blister, and recalled that the aircraft had been built by Boeing for the US Navy and then, when the war was over, delivered to the Royal Australian Navy who had sold it on to Barrier Reef Airways.

Our launch came up alongside the plane. It was time to board.

Many hands assisted Mum as she made a wobbly transition from launch to aircraft.

The flying boat's captain helped us board. 'G'day,' he said. 'Make yourselves comfortable. Our flight to Heron Island takes two hours and twenty minutes. If any of you are taken short we have a dunny. It will be high tide at Heron in a hour, so we have plenty of time to spare.' He turned to my mother, lowered his voice and added 'I hope you have time to spare?'

Mum grinned. 'They tell me I'm good for another month,' she replied.

'Good on you,' said the captain. 'No worries. We'll have you there and back by then.'

I was too busy admiring the luxurious interior of the Catalina to wonder what my mother meant. I had just stepped into a wartime patrol bomber recently refurbished to airliner standards by Barrier Reef Airways.

I was in heaven.

What comfort!

There were adjustable, upholstered seats for twenty-two passengers in three separate, lined compartments.

My parents, Annie, Claws and I had the smallest of these three cabins all to ourselves.

I squeezed past Mum to the window seat, whipped out my notebook and my 2B drawing pencil, and went to work.

I was an artist.

I sketched away. I did not want to miss a thing.

My Mum had taught me how to draw by *not* teaching me.

She had let me see her drawing things. I had noted how she had taken on a serious, abstracted air, and had begun to sketch without even looking down at her pencil.

By watching her work I had learned to see for myself the lines in whatever was before me and to put those lines down on paper. I planned to go out on the reef with my notebook when we reached Heron Island. I planned to gaze into coral pools at low tide and draw the wonders of nature: sea stars, sea urchins and bêche-de-mer. I imagined that strange shellfish might prance by on tiptoes.

I might even feast my eyes on a Giant Clam. What a prospect! I couldn't wait. Soon we would be there!

I hadn't the foggiest notion that getting there might be fraught with peril, nor that I might have to risk my life.

Happily I sucked the end of my pencil. I decided to draw the flying boat. When drawing a flying boat the first thing is to decide is whether or not to draw the plane floating in the water or flying through the air.

I decided on flying through the air. That way I could show the whole fuselage and put in some fiddly details.

First I had to get the general shape right. That was easy. The bottom of a flying boat is shaped like a whale. One of Dad's better stories about Sponge, X and Y had involved a whale who carried an island on his back. I had drawn that whale before, so I knew the right shape: streamlined yet bulbous, with clear, curving lines sweeping up to the tail.

The whale in Dad's stories was called - you guessed it - the Island Whale.

I drew the island on top of my whale.

Although it was hard work for Dad's whale swimming about with an island on his back, the island was worth it.

It was home to a hobgoblin and nine monkeys.

The names of Dad's nine monkeys were Number One Monkey, Number Two Monkey, Number Three Monkey, Number Four Monkey, Number Five Monkey, Number Six Monkey, Number Seven Monkey, Number Eight Monkey and Number Nine Monkey.

I drew them all.

My favourite was Number Seven Monkey. Whenever the hobgoblin waved his magic boot, Number Seven Monkey turned into Supermonkey.

'Sideways and away!' Supermonkey would say, and then he would fly up, up into the sky.

By the time I had finished drawing Supermonkey, with his cloak flying out behind him, and the hobgoblin waving his magic boot, and the nine palm trees, one for each monkey, there was no room left on the page for the *Beachcomber*.

I turned to a fresh page. I began again.

I decided to portray the plane differently this time.

I would draw her just after taking off from the water. I sketched in the sweeping curve of her hull, narrowing, diminishing aft, and then rising sharply up to her tail. She was flying toward the left hand side of my page.

I added the pilot's cockpit near the nose of the plane. I put in the captain and the copilot staring forward anxiously through the windscreen. They were anxious to get to Heron Island.

Right behind the pilots in their flight deck I drew the twin propeller engines.

I gave each propeller three blades. The engines were 1,200 horsepower each. Drawing the wings was tricky, for the near wing had to look bigger.

I used my rubber a lot to get the perspective right. Once I had the wings in place, I joined the wings to the fuselage by means of a streamlined pedestal shaped like the conning tower of a submarine.

To make that arrangement strong enough I added vertical ribs and spars on both sides joining the wings to the fuselage of the *Beachcomber*.

I drew the blister bulging out of the side of the plane.

I drew a fierce gunner inside the blister.

I spent some time drawing the end of the wing nearest to the right hand side of the page with the under-wing float in the *down* position. I had to make sure that someone looking at my drawing would understand that when folded *up* out of the way the float would extend the wing by two feet. Both floats added four extra feet to the overall wingspan, making it one hundred and four feet from wingtip to wingtip.

I thought this was neat.

The under-wing float, lowered for takeoff and landing on water became a wingtip once the *Beachcomber* was in the air! The engineer who dreamed that up deserved a prize.

I finished off my rendition by adding the aircraft identification letters VH-BRA to the tail and drew a winged roundel with the letters BRA on a white seabird's wing and two palm trees bent over by the wind clinging to an island of coral sand standing out against a vivid blue sky. This I copied from the Barrier Reef Airways luggage sticker on my satchel.

I was pleased with my picture. I stared at it and imagined being in the cockpit and flying the plane myself. I could almost feel the thrumming of the engines. I glanced down at my pilot's watch which I wore upside down with its dial facing upwards on the *inside* of my wrist as I was sure a true pilot would. I dreamed that I was serving in Biggles's squadron. *I had been in the air for about fifty minutes. The stars were winking out one by one. I was nearing Berglaken. I saw ahead of me Biggles's Camel sinking into the void. He had cut his engine! I reached for the throttle of my own machine. I pushed the joystick forward.*

The horizon disappeared. My vertical speed indicator was indicating a descent of 10,000 feet per minute. My airspeed indicator was in the yellow 200 knots zone. It was time to level off and pull out of the dive. I gingerly eased back on the control. My feet steadily kept an even pressure to avoid an incipient spin.

I began to lose height.

The ground came rushing towards me.

I saw lakes connected by a canal. At the last moment I straightened out. My VSI gave a positive rate of climb. An old aviator's adage came to mind: Aviate, Navigate, Communicate. I saw archie bursts and star shells...

'Are you hungry?' asked Mum, interrupting my reverie. 'I believe they will be serving a tropical salad later.'

'I'm all right for now, thanks,' I said, dragging myself back to the real world.

I was not entirely fond of the real world.

In the real world I was just a passenger.

In the real world the flight crew would be warding off their enemies without any help from me. They had better put up a good show.

I was a Biggles enthusiast.

Although the war was long over, I hoped nobody had told the Germans in Colmslie.

I thirsted for adventure.

I was about to get more than I bargained for.

2: Takeoff

THE CAPTAIN of the *Beachcomber* paused at my seat to have a look at my drawing. 'That's pretty spiffy,' he said.

'Thanks,' I replied, beaming with pride. 'Why are the wings so high up?' I asked, recalling a picture of a seaplane with wings attached underneath, not on top.

'We like to keep our wings dry.' The captain gave me a wink and then moved on down the cabin to say 'G'day' to his other passengers.

'He's hiding something,' I whispered to Annie.

Annie was my drama director.

She knew to bring my daydreams to life.

I had read enough books by Captain W. E. Johns to know that the skies were filled with air pirates, barrage balloons and enemy machines. Our chances of reaching Heron Island must be slim indeed.

'Our mission is to pick up an escaped prisoner of war,' I suggested.

Biggles *always* had a mission.

Annie's face lit up. 'Good. As soon as we're up in the air, I'll shout "We're all going to die!" and then I'll froth at the mouth.'

I was stunned. 'Can you really? Froth at the mouth?'

Annie was happy to demonstrate. Boy, could she froth! Her mother is a famous actress. They probably froth three times a day.

'What about me? What do I do?' I asked, feeling a little upstaged.

'You look noble. You say in a deep voice "Everything is going to be all right, Annie," and then you brush a tear from your cheek to let the audience know you are lying.'

I was about to say this when to our considerable alarm and deeply felt joy the din of the aircraft's engines suddenly swelled and became enormous, and our seats shook.

The flying boat was preparing to take off, or to explode. It was hard to tell which.

'JUST TESTING THE ENGINES!' I mouthed at Annie, and wiped an invisible tear from my cheek.

Annie replied with Faye Wray meets King Kong.

'WE ARE ALL GOING TO DIE!' she shouted back happily.

I grinned.

Annie was all right.

I was careful not to look at Claws. I disliked Claws.

I wished Claws had not come.

If Claws had been sitting in an ejection seat, I would have hit the button.

The aircraft began to move.

I had the window seat. I pressed my nose to the glass and looked out. This was my first time in a plane. I could feel the vibrations of the huge engines as the captain began to throttle up for takeoff. The machine heaved. We were floating. I could see the water going up and down.

As the VH-BRA Catalina flying boat *Beachcomber* nosed slowly through the waves, I tried to puzzle out what the letters VH-BRA stood for. Surely the BR stood for Barrier Reef, and the A meant she was the first in the Barrier Reef Airways fleet, but what did the VH stand for? Very Happy? Very Hoppy? She was certainly hopping happily over the waves.

I spied the harbour launch making her way back to the dock through the heat haze. That made sense.

I had grown used to harbours and docks while travelling with my parents in the RMS *Orcades* to this strange and wonderful land of Oz. I had read up on Oz in the ship's library. I had yet to see my first munchkin, which I regretted, but there had been no sign of the Wicked Witch either, for which I was thankful.

During our voyage to Oz Annie and I had become fast friends and Claws had become our sworn enemy.

Grown-ups being incapable of making such distinctions, both Annie *and* Claws had been invited to join me on my holiday excursion to Heron Island. That was why both Annie and Claws were sharing this cabin of *Beachcomber* with me and with my parents.

I sighed.

Parents! There was just no accounting for them. Mum and Dad had meant well in inviting Claws along. They always meant well. It was the consequences I had to live with.

I puffed up my cheeks in resignation and returned my attention to the water sliding past my window.

At any moment, I was to be carried up into the air! This was for real! This was now!

I exhaled.

I stared earnestly at the under-wing float.

It was shaped like a little boat.

The float was attached to the end of the wing by a wide sturdy metal strut. I watched it skim the crest of wave after wave and was amazed to see that it left furrows behind just like a flying fish. It was fun to watch that float bounce along. It was a sight I would long remember.

I was thrilled to pieces when the mighty Twin Wasp radial engines took on an even more serious note and the entire aircraft began to shake.

Annie and I looked at each other, scared and excited. She did not look at Claws. I did not look at Claws. We shared this moment, just the two of us, Annie and me.

The engines grew louder.

Annie's eyes grew wider.

The flying boat began to slam into wave crest after wave crest. I could feel the plane trying desperately to get up out of the sea and into the air. She was straining and straining. Would she succeed? Or would we all die? It was touch and go.

Shaken out of stowage, a bag belonging to a member of the Heron Island Research Station staff rolled into the aisle and burst open.

A giant shell tumbled out.

Annie and I watched with growing horror as the shell righted itself and began to climb slowly, relentlessly up the slope. It was headed for the flight deck! It lurched from side to side. It waved pincers. It was alive. It was going to take over the plane.

We were transfixed. This was better than anything we had dared hoped for. This was wicked. This was gruesome. Who would be the first to die?

Annie's eyes were now as round as saucers.

I clenched my fists.

God help the pilots! The shell was coming to get them.

It was huge.

It had spiny legs.

Both Annie and I knew what to expect next.

Before leaving for Heron Island, Annie and I had taken a tram to the Odeon Cinema in Melbourne. We had paid sixpence each to see a horror film called Ghost Ship.

So we knew that this giant shell crawling up the aisle was but the grim beginning to a parade of ghastly terrors.

Half-eaten bodies would be discovered, and then someone would go completely nuts and rush through the cabin screaming, and all the passengers would panic.

Annie and me were filled with depraved glee at this prospect. We could hardly wait for the mayhem to break out. This was going to be a flight to remember.

Dragging my eyes from the ominous shell, I turned back to look out of the window.

The under-wing float was bouncing about like a mad thing. Suddenly the bow wave of the flying boat's hull covered my window with churning white seawater. It was as if I were inside a Speed Queen 40 electric wringer washer.

The growing thunder of the engines and the crash, crash, crash of the bow of the plane hitting the wave crests rose to a deafening crescendo.

I gripped the arms of my seat.

I braced myself.

Dinky-di!

I knew from my extensive readings of the adventures of Squadron Leader James Bigglesworth that on the flight deck, located forward of the engines, our captain would be advancing the throttle controls to their full forward position for takeoff.

His copilot would be mopping the sweat from his forehead and craning his neck to scan the sky for German triplanes. *Always keep an eye on the sky. The enemy is never far away.*

'The shell!' I wanted to shout out to the pilots. 'Look out! Behind you!'

I risked a quick glance at Claws to see if he, too, had spotted the shell humping its way up the aisle. He had. He was squinting at it with his piggy little eyes.

I clenched my fists.

Claws had no right to be here spoiling our holiday. I would finish him off at the earliest opportunity. I would bring him down with a returning wave kick followed by a scissor punch.

I had read about how to do this in a book.

The book had many helpful diagrams. If the returning wave kick and scissor punch combination did not work, there were sixteen other ways to kill Claws.

The captain and copilot had left the door to the flight deck open. The careless fools!

I gripped the armrests of my seat.

The colossal reverberation of the aircraft rose to a mid-numbing skull-rattling climax and then to my surprise the deafening roar of the engines and the thumping of the wave crests ceased abruptly and were replaced in an instant by a subdued, confident drone.

Annie and I were stunned.

We were still alive.

We had taken off.

The Catalina's engines were in their natural element.

We were airborne.

As the water drained from the outside of my window, turning into hundreds of little bobbles, and those bobbles scurried aft, the glass cleared and I saw for the first time the coastline of Queensland spread out below me as clear as day.

I gulped.

The land was far away!

We were high up in the air.

We were flying.

I was flying.

And the shell was still crawling up the aisle towards the flight deck.

Our captain and our copilot were in danger.

I was no stranger to danger.

Upon my our arrival in Oz, my parents had

enrolled me in a Dickensian school named Grimwade House where every morning at assembly we had gathered dressed in our sweltering blazers to sing a song of unfathomable dangers:

> *Play together, Dark Blue Twenty,*
> *Long and little marks in plenty;*
> *Get your kick, let none prevent ye,*
> *Make the leather roll.*

I had soon learned that *making the leather roll* was about the danger of having shoes thrown at you by your mathematics teacher, and that the *long and little marks in plenty* were inflicted by Claws and his gang during lunch hour.

I had been a day pupil.

Every day had become more dangerous than the last.

Claws and his cronies had eyed my lunchbox.

Every morning my Mum had packed me a lunchbox with delicious sandwiches and a treat called Sweetacres Jaffa that had a chocolate core and an orange-tasting shell.

Sweetacres Jaffa was my favourite. I had liked to munch on Sweetacres Jaffa while watching Flash Gordon and other Saturday morning serials at the Odeon. Sometimes Mum had been kind enough to slip into my lunchbox a packet of Smith's Potato Crisps. What Mum had not known was that Grimwade House was so dangerous I had never had a chance to eat *anything* she put in my lunchbox.

Every morning as I stepped off the tram and entered the school grounds, Claws and his gang had snatched my lunch box. Day after day they had run off with it, laughing. Claws had enjoyed making smaller boys miserable. He and his gang were bigger than I was. I had been unable to think of any practical way to prevent them from taking my lunch box, though why they had wanted to take it I had found sorely puzzling.

Perhaps Claws had a mother who was too poor to pack a lunch for him? Perhaps he missed his father?

I had refused to be seen to cry.

Instead I had spent my hungry lunch breaks in the school library reading about body slams, drop kicks, and pile drivers and planning what I would do to Claws if ever I had him to myself.

I had a good mind to give Claws one for his nob and put him out for good.

At the end of my school day ducking the flying shoes, I had rummaged in the rubbish bins in search of my empty discarded lunch box. Claws and his cronies liked to put my lunch box a different bin every day and to cover it with as much rubbish as possible.

Only after all the other boys had left had I given way to tears. I had cried for my mother. She had gone to all that trouble on my behalf, and I felt I had let her down.

It did not seem fair on *her*.

That was what made me cry.

Then, when I had dried my eyes, I had taken the tram home. Trams in Melbourne do not stop for children. They assume you have no money to pay your fare. So I had had to jump on. The tram had come racing towards me, spitting and crackling and hopping about, and I had leaped onto the boarding platform and grabbed for the handrail. If I had missed the handrail, I would have died.

I repeat: I was no stranger to danger.

And now that awful shell was making its way towards the cockpit.

I looked at Annie.
Annie looked at me.
We had to be brave.
We had to save the *Beachcomber*.

3: Crabbing Along

'THE SHELL,' I said.

Annie leapt from her adjustable and upholstered seat. I squeezed past Mum. We had to save the pilots.

Annie and I raced up the sloping aisle.

We fell upon the monstrous shell.

We held onto the shell tightly but the conch would not stop. It was immensely powerful and fiercely determined. It continued on up the aisle towards the cockpit, dragging us both after it.

What to do?

If both pilots were clawed to death by this lurching monster of a shell, who would be left to fly the plane? My Dad was in the Navy, not the Air Force. He knew nothing of flying.

I knew what I would have to do. I would have to fly the plane myself. I had read thirty-five and a half Biggles books. Flying the *Beachcomber* would be a piece of cake.

Annie would be my copilot. I would ask Annie to get on the radio and warn Heron Island we were coming. We would send out a mayday. We would be a sensation!

Fame beckoned.

I could see the headline:

Boy and Girl Save Plane!

Annie and I would ham it up at the medal ceremony.

'It was nothing,' we would say in unison to the flashing cameras. 'We are no heroes' we would chorus, knowing full well that we were the bravest of the brave.

As we told our lies to the press we would exchange secret, knowing smiles.

We would become the stuff of legend.

But that was in the future, and this was the present. Right now we were in a jam. How were we to save the pilots? The conch with which we were struggling was rough on the outside but smooth and pearly pink on the inside. We could feel it digging in its claws in as it hauled us along.

The shell we were holding trembled!

'Do you feel that?' said Annie.

I nodded, speechless.

Something inside the shell had smelled the pilots! I thought I heard the beast sharpening its claws.

We should all be torn to bits.

I had no trouble at all imagining the *Beachcomber* crabbing along, a derelict flying boat filled with gnawed skeletons.

A ghost ship!

'Be careful please. That shell is home to *Dardanus deformis*.'

We looked up.

A grown-up lady was speaking to us.

'You may call me Dr. B,' she said. 'I'm a biologist at the Heron Island research station.'

Annie and I exchanged knowing glances. There had been a scientist in the film Ghost Ship. We well remembered what had happened to *her*.

We examined this real-life scientist carefully from head to toe.

Yes, she was definitely on the menu. She looked delicious. She had smooth peachy cheeks and thin, crunchy bones. We did not listen to a word she was saying. We were too busy wondering which bit of her would be nibbled off first.

A nose?

An ear?

'Dardanus was a warrior king who lost his helmet while battling the Bebrycians,' Dr. B informed us. 'Dardanus's troops were retreating, but Dardanus insisted they go back to find his helmet. They went back to look for it and won the battle.'

Annie and I were filled with despair.

What a shame that this yummy doctor had to die!

It was no good trying to warn her. Grown-ups have only a limited understanding of the world, and it is a complete waste of time talking to them about ghost ships. Believe me, I have tried.

We were on Dr. B's side, nonetheless.

Had there been any way to persuade this confident and eminently edible scientist that *all* of our lives were in danger, and that this tottering zombie shell was but the first of a string of horrors soon to come, then we would have done so.

Alas, the good doctor had not seen the film, or, if she had seen it, she had not taken it seriously. Many adults perish for want of imagination.

To our surprise Dr. B. grabbed the great shell from us and lifted it high into the air.

'*Dardanus deformis* is a hermit crab,' she told us. 'The shell does not belong to him. He found it lying about and decided it would make a pleasant, safe place to live. Now you have come along and spoiled his plans.'

Yuck!

I could see the crab's ten legs waving!

The crab was opening a closing its pincers!

'And you are?'

'Anthony Barton,' I whispered.

'Annie Lamarr,' said Annie.

'Well, Anthony and Annie, if you would care to help me put this hermit crab back in its bag then I promise that when we arrive at Heron Island, I shall invite you to witness the return of the lost warrior and his helmet to the reef.'

We stifled our fears and provided nominal assistance to Dr. B as she put the kicking monster safely back into captivity.

We were heartbroken. Poor Dr. B!

Before long, parts of her would be missing: an eyeball, or half an arm. We knew this to be true. We had seen the film. We watched in unmitigated gloom as the doctor closed and latched the door of the cage.

'What's a reef?' asked Annie, puzzled.

'Let me show you,' said the scrumptious biologist, and she led us to the rear of the plane.

She rummaged in a storage bin. She handed us lumps of dead white coral. 'That's what a reef is made of,' she explained.

My bit of coral felt hard and brittle.

It had little sharp edges.

'Why all the holes?' I asked, turning the lump over in my hands warily.

'Every one of those small holes was once home to a sea creature the size of a pinhead,' Dr. B replied.

'We call the sea creature a polyp,' she went on. 'Each polyp built walls of limestone around itself to protect itself from its enemies. Each polyp had babies. After each polyp died, it left its little home vacant.'

'And then her babies built themselves new homes?' asked Annie brightly, putting on her interested-student face.

'And the reef grew bigger?' I said, anxious not to be left out.

'Stupid polyps,' said a familiar voice from behind us.

Annie and I spun around.

'Claws!' said Annie.

Claws looked like an ordinary boy but we knew him to be a bully and a ghost. Worse, he was the reincarnation of my pet cat.

I did not know why my cat had taken on the form of this cruel, lunch-swiping boy.

That was a mystery.

Suffice to say that Annie and I knew Claws to be evil. Three weeks ago he had thrown our library books into the sea.

In consequence Annie had never found out what had happened to the Famous Five and their secret dog, and I had never learned what had become of Biggles after he had become trapped behind enemy lines.

You don't get much more evil than that.

I suspected Claws was trying to get back at me for not bringing him with me to Oz.

Meow.

'We meet again, Mr. Claws,' I said coldly in my best Biggles voice.

Claws brought his heels together.

He bowed formally.

'Anthony,' he said, and then turned and clicked his heels together again.

'Annie.'

He held out his hand.

We knew better than to take his hand.

Never shake hands with a cat.

'The polyps are not stupid, Claws,' I said, correcting him. 'They built the Great Barrier Reef. The reef is 1,250 miles long. My Dad told me.'

'Reef home to stonefish,' said Claws. 'Stonefish kill you.'

'What's a stonefish?' asked Annie, turning to the delectable doctor.

Dr. B cleared her throat. 'The reef stonefish, *Synanceia verrucosa*, is a foot long. The fish has thirteen dorsal fin spines that inject you with deadly venom. Never tread on a stonefish. Your friend is right to warn you. I have a stonefish in my luggage.'

My mind raced.

She has a stonefish in her luggage.

What else do you have in your luggage, Doctor B?

'Claws is not our friend. He is our enemy,' I said solemnly.

I did not tell her that not long ago Annie and I had risked our lives to save Claws during a storm.

He was our enemy, but we hadn't wanted him to die *by accident*.

Instead we had a grim end planned for him.

The doctor looked puzzled.

She was out of her depth.

I felt for her.

It is not easy being an adult.

Most adults are pitiful creatures who need

the help of young people and have to be shielded from the harsher realties of life.

The doctor regarded us curiously. 'Return to your seats,' she ordered. 'Keep the bits of coral. Here is a piece for you,' she added, and handed Claws a fragment. She was trying to be fair.

I ran back to our seats and showed my chunk of coral to my mother.

'Dr. B says Heron Island is made of stuff like this,' I explained. 'Things live in the holes.'

'*The Microbe is so very small you cannot make him out at all,*' said Mum.

'I don't know that one,' I said.

'It's from *More Beasts for Worse Children* by Hilaire Belloc,' she said, returning my chunk of coral to me for safekeeping.

'It's true. I can't make them out at all,' I said, turning the coral over in my hands. 'Tell me another.'

'*The moon on the one hand, the dawn on the other: the moon is my sister, the dawn is my brother. The moon on my left and the dawn on my right. My brother, good morning: my sister, good night.*'

'Who is that by?'

'The same poet, Hilaire Belloc. It is called The Early Morning.'

I basked in that verse for a moment. It sounded so tidy. *My brother good morning: my sister, good night.* I wondered what it would be like to have a sister.

I shivered. I had a vague premonition of disaster.

'If I had a sister, what would she be called?'

'Miranda.'

'*Never more, Miranda, never more? Only the high peaks hoar and Aragon a torrent at the door?* That one?'

'Yes.'

'Miranda.' I tried out the name, rolling it around on my tongue. 'Miranda, Miranda.'

Something was definitely up.

Had Mum been trying to get through to the Land of the Dead again?

'What was my grandmother like?' I asked.

'Your grandmother made woodcuts. She made a woodcut of me when I was three, holding a bowl of fruit. I had to stand there in her draughty studio in my best yellow dress.'

A woodblock of my mother
fashioned by my grandmother
Mabel Allington Royds

When she wasn't making woodblocks, Mabel made porcelain dolls and cut out clothes for them. She sewed on tiny buttons and made tiny buttonholes. She sold her dolls to help pay the rent. She sewed that little red coat for your bear.'

'For Whitey?'

Mum nodded.

'You want to sew dresses for Miranda,' I said flatly.

I was furious.

I felt betrayed.

An angel passed.

I stared at Mum.

Mum stared back at me.

I heard the singsong words of *Tarantella* jangling in my mind:

Do you remember an Inn,
Miranda?
Do you remember an Inn?
And the tedding and the spreading
Of the straw for a bedding...

Sensing that something was wrong between us, Dad looked up from his book *Wonders of the Great Barrier Reef* by T. C. Roughley.

'On Heron Island,' he said, 'we shall be allowed to walk out on the reef at low tide and see many amazing creatures trapped in the coral pools.'

'Which creature do you want to see the most?' I asked.

'Most of all I'm looking forward to meeting the green turtle. In my book it says an adult green turtle is four feet long and weighs five hundred pounds.'

Five hundred pounds! That sounded like rather a lot of turtle.

I shared my Dad's excitement. Back in England I had once fed lettuce leaves to a pet tortoise I called Slobadob.

I had watched Slobadob devour each leaf slowly and deliberately, with the ponderous dignity of an herbivorous dinosaur.

Slobadob had been all of ten inches long, and quite heavy to lift. To pick him up I had had to use both my hands.

If Dad's book was right, then the Heron Island turtles were much heavier.

I hoped we would see one.

'What's the difference between a tortoise and a turtle?' I asked, on the principle that one should try one's best to ask one's parents simple questions to which they are likely to know the answers.

'A turtle likes to swim,' was my father's reply.

'Can a turtle walk at all?'

'Yes. The female turtle drags herself up onto the land to lay and bury her eggs. She does this at night. At this time of year we can watch a green turtle lay her eggs on the beach at Heron Island. You may have to stay up late and use your electric torch.'

Staying up late sounded good, and I was dying to try out my electric torch.

Miranda was forgotten. My mind was crawling with turtles instead. I had been well and truly distracted.

'*Will you, won't you, will you, won't you, will you join the dance?*' said Mum.

'*Alice's Adventures in Wonderland*,' I said.

She nodded. 'The Queen asks Alice "Have you seen the Mock Turtle yet?" and Alice replies "No, I don't even know what a Mock Turtle is." Then the Queen tells her "It's the thing Mock Turtle Soup is made from" and she takes Alice to meet the Mock Turtle. "Once," says the Mock Turtle "I was a real Turtle" and then he bursts into tears.'

'Poor Mock Turtle,' I said, and took a deep breath. Grown-up conversation was so tedious.

I had to make my escape.

'I want to go to the dunny,' I said.

4: Dead Stick

'THE CAPTAIN said the facility was portside aft.'

'No worries. I'll find it.'

The dunny was inside the gun blister.

I drew the curtain.

I sat on the Elsan.

I was inside the gun blister, a transparent dome that stuck out of the side of the plane.

I was floating along in the heavens.

I could look down and see the sea.

I could look up and see the sky.

When we flew inside a cloud I became Dan Dare, Pilot of the Future, crossing the equatorial cloud belt of Venus to battle green-skinned Treens and meet their brainy leader the Mekon floating through the air on his own little flying boat.

It was smashing.

I sat there for ages and ages.

I was as happy as a lark sitting on the Elsan in the *Beachcomber*'s gun blister.

Then I saw the stick.

The stick lay beside the washbasin.

It was just an ordinary stick.

But there was something funny about it.

Something very odd.

The stick was thirteen inches long. I supposed that somebody had left the stick lying by the soap dish. It was just a dead stick. So I thought.

And then I saw the dead stick move.

Very slowly, very carefully, the stick came to life. Three pairs of long spindly legs lifted the stick off the ground and carried it along jerkily like a man balancing on stilts. From the forward end of the dead stick, two long antennae protruded, feeling the way ahead. They discovered the soap dish.

The living stick turned and walked towards me. Greatly daring, I put out a finger. The walking stick touched my finger with one antenna, and froze.

It thought about my finger for a long time.

I kept still.

The stick insect kept still.

I said nothing.

The stick insect said nothing.

I waited.

The stick insect came back to life.

The stick insect climbed up on my finger.

The stick insect walked right up my arm. It was a fearless. It was a creature of Oz. I had met my munchkin. Its little feet were tickly.

Very carefully I transferred the creature to the counter on the other side of the washbasin.

The stick stalked off, managing its long limbs with admirable deftness.

I returned to our cabin ecstatic and gave a thumbs up to Annie who lost no time in visiting the gun blister for herself, and returned with her eyes dancing.

Claws saw the looks we were exchanging and dashed to the back of the plane to try out the Elsan.

'If he sees the walking stick, he'll pull its legs off,' I whispered.

'I hid the creature out of sight behind the spare rolls of lavatory paper,' said Annie.

'Good for you,' I said. 'Claws is *not* to be trusted.'

My mother looked at us both and frowned.

She lowered her voice and spoke reprovingly. 'I don't know how much you two know about Klaus. That is his real name, Klaus, by the way. You should learn to say his name properly like this: "Klows." It is not respectful of you to call him Claws. Klaus is short for Nikolaus. His family fled from the Nazis during the war.'

Annie and I exchanged glances.

We were not sure who the Nasties were, but we thought it a shame that Claws had got away from them.

Mum went on: 'You do recall that Klaus's father died on the *Orcades* because of his mistreatment at Auschwitz? His poor mother would have loved to come with us to Heron Island but she would have lost her job if she had. The government in Australia does not approve of immigrant women with no husband to support them.'

'But Mum, you don't understand. Claws is not really a boy.' I lowered my voice. 'He destroyed our library books.'

Mum shook her head sadly. 'I hear you locked him in the Children's Playroom in the *Orcades* all by himself. That wasn't very nice. How do you think he felt about that?'

Annie and I stared down at our shoes.

We did not know what to say.

How is it that grown-ups come to know *everything*?

My mother read our faces. She relented. 'Klaus saw all sorts of horrid things during the war, and he is scared. You would be scared too if you were he.'

Mum waggled her finger at us. 'You would be frightened out of your wits if you had been through half of what he has been through. Your father and I are taking Klaus to Heron Island to cheer him up. So be civil to him. Play with him. Invite him to take part in your games. Do you think you can do that?'

Annie and I risked a quick exchange of looks.

We were embarrassed. We squirmed. Mum made it sound as if we were the villains, when we knew for a fact that Claws was the most dreadful villain in the entire universe. If Claws had suffered so much in the war, it was high time to put him out of his misery. Permanently.

'We'll do our best,' I said, affecting an air of resignation and capitulation while planning to murder Claws as soon as possible.

Annie did the Annunciation to the Blessed Virgin.

She stared up at my mother as if she were Gabriel.

Her eyes filled with tears.

Tears on demand!

Annie's performance was so moving she brought tears to *my* eyes.

Mum was a little taken aback by our waterworks. 'You just have to be kind to him, that's all I'm asking.'

Annie nodded, and put on a brave show of fighting back her stage tears. Boy, Annie was good.

Do actors ever stop acting?

Claws came back from his visit to the dunny baring his teeth in an evil grin.

I wondered what he had done there that had made him so happy.

Jumped up and down on the stick insect?

I looked at Claws in a new light.

So his real name was Klaus. Who cared?

What could this horrible boy have seen during the war that had been so ghastly?

I found that I was eager to hear about all of the horrors and suffering he had endured.

I was as wicked he was.

I wanted to steal his lunchbox.

I wanted to hide his lunchbox in rubbish.

Play together Dark Blue Twenty...

A flash of lightning lit up our cabin.

It was time. I squeezed past Mum. 'Want to see a stonefish, Claws?'

Annie and I led Claws into the darkest corner of Dr. B's menagerie where the grown-ups could not see us.

'Vere is stonefish?' said Claws, peering down into the tank.

I clicked on my electric torch and sent a beam of light down into the murky depths.

A strange frilly shape, dotted with orange and red spots, stared back at us with a baleful eye.

A wide mouth opened and closed.

We glimpsed bejewelled fins. We saw venomous dorsal spines.

'Stupid fish,' said Claws.

'What did you see in the war?' I whispered. 'Bet you didn't see anything.'

'You don't have to say if you don't want to,' said Annie.

The light of my torch bounced off the aquarium and lit up his face from underneath.

It was a scene from Ghost Ship.

Claws stared off into the darkness.

His face went blank.

I wanted to curl up and die.

'What did you see, Claws?'

It was cruel to ask Claws about the war.

But I asked him anyway. I was that bad.

'Ven we arrive,' he said slowly 'zey make us go different places. My sister go to slave labour, my parents sent off one vay, my brothers go other vay. I am thinking 'Vere is sister?'

Annie and I froze.

Claws had had brothers and sisters!

'Don't tell us any more,' I said.

'They march us through snow. No clothes.'

'That's enough. Sorry I asked.'

Annie gave Claws a hug.

Claws looked surprised.

Perhaps nobody had ever hugged him before.

'Stupid snow,' he said in a whisper, and I saw that his cheek was wet.

I had made Claws cry.

I could not meet Annie's eyes.

What had I done?

What had we done?

What was death anyway? How did it work? What did you feel? What happened afterwards?

Was there an afterwards?

Did anyone know?

I didn't know.

Dad came looking for us.

'Come and eat,' he said cheerfully. 'Tropical salad. They don't have a galley on the *Beachcomber* so the copilot's wife Hope has prepared ready-to-eat meals for us. You'll need a spoon.'

We returned to our cabin and ate our meals in silence. It was a relief to have something ordinary to do. My tropical salad had slices of mango in it. I had never tasted mango before. It was cool and sweet and wonderful.

I was sorry for Claws. My own war years had been a bit on the hungry side. Mum and Dad had both served in the navy. They had refused to cheat on rations. We had gone without. We had lived in a married quarters hut with a pot-bellied stove to keep us warm and a sheepdog called Woolly to hug. My family had not been torn apart by the war. I had not seen death.

I had not, to my knowledge, lost any brothers or sisters in the conflict, or been marched though snow.

Include Klaus in your games.

After we had finished our tropical salads, I sacrificed three as yet unused pages from my notebook, distributed pencils, and suggested 'Heads, Bodies and Legs.' This was the first time Annie and I had invited Claws to play with us.

We divided each page into three equal parts. Then we drew a head in the first third of the paper, making sure our head included two lines for the neck extending down into the middle part of the page.

I drew the head of a walrus and gave my walrus two tusks and a look of bemused innocence.

I folded my paper to hide the walrus from prying eyes.

'Time!' said Annie, after she had put the finishing touches to whatever kind of head she had drawn. She folded her own paper carefully to hide her sketch.

'Stupid pencil,' said Claws, still slaving away.

At last Claws finished what he was drawing and folded his paper.

'Pass!' said Annie, and we passed the folded sheets along.

I passed mine to Claws.

Claws passed his sheet to Annie.

Annie passed hers to me.

I could not see what sort of head Annie had drawn, but I could see her extended neck lines waiting for me, and they were wide apart, so I drew the body of Crybaby Corby the wrestler. Then I folded Crybaby out of sight and passed the paper on to Claws to finish the picture.

Annie passed her folded sheet to me.

Claws passed his folded sheet to Annie.

All three of use went back to work, and this time we drew the legs.

I drew the legs of a wallaby. When we were all done, it was time to unfold the three sheets and see what kind of strange monsters we had created between us.

They were hilarious!

A stonefish with wings stomping around in suede leather brown boots!

An officer of the Schutzstaffel hopping about like a wallaby!

The Wicked Witch of the West pirouetting on ballet shoes!

Annie and I had a fit of giggles.

Claws managed a small smile.

Had I been wrong about Claws?

Was Claws human after all?

Naaah.

He was a dead stick. He had come to life. He was stalking along, feeling about for a soap dish.

We had done as my mother had asked. We had invited Claws to join us in a game.

Now we could kill him with a clear conscience.

5: Nothing On The Clock

OUR PLANE was in trouble. I could see pellets of ice jumping about on the wings, lit up by St. Elmo's fire. An ominous golden glow surrounded the entire leading edge of the wing.

Flocks of strange Oz pigeons with bronze wings wheeled through the sky in dizzying circles. The birds knew something bad was coming.

Dr. B's cages began to rattle.

I heard something with tentacles dance a mad quadrille and a hiss as a bulbous bogie swelled up like a balloon.

Thunder shook the plane.

My pilot's watch stopped.

I shook my wrist.

My watch started again.

More thunder.

If this was a Biggles book, what would the pilots be doing?

On the flight deck the pilots would be busy going through their check list, disengaging autopilot as they entered the storm, re-setting the directional gyrocompass and advancing the mix control all the way to the firewall. The air would be much thinner up here with less oxygen.

Would Dr. B's creatures survive?

'They are being experimented on,' I had whispered.

Annie had responded by narrowing her eyes, and lifting her chin. 'All that we do, we do in the name of science.'

Claws had given one of the specimen cages a savage kick and had crowed when the inhabitant of the cage had flung itself to and fro in a desperate effort to escape. 'Stupid fish!' he had said.

'Do that again, Claws,' I had said, 'and I'll give you an eagle-beak.'

'You and who else?' Claws had jeered.

'Him and me,' Annie had retorted. 'Leave the beasts alone. They don't like being in cages. You wouldn't like it if somebody kicked your cage.'

'Like this?' Claws had said, and he had kicked another.

A yellow-skinned thing with eight arms and blue and black rings had responded by grabbing Claws's ankle.

Annie and I had looked at one another.

We had been confused about what to do.

Were we to let Claws suffer, or try to rescue him?

'*Autsch!*' Claws had said, his eyes watering. He had shaken his foot angrily, trying to rid himself of his determined attacker. 'Vot is this?' he had asked.

'It's an octopus,' Annie had said quietly. 'Don't frighten it. The ones with blue rings are dangerous.'

On hearing Annie say this, I had become alarmed.

Suppose Claws died of his own foolishness?

Who then would I practice my ox-jaw hand strike on?

I was so looking forward to the applause of an admiring crowd.

So there had been nothing for it but to attempt some kind of a rescue.

Keeping a wary eye on the octopus's venomous beak, I had tickled the animal.

'Don't make me laugh,' I had said to the octopus.

I had stroked the octopus's mantle.

I had fondled the octopus's eye bumps.

I had lost all sense of proportion.

I had risked my own life to save Claws!

The octopus had relaxed and let go.

I had slipped the octopus back into its cage. It had been shy. I had done what I could to refasten the damaged door of its home.

Of course I should have let the octopus finish off Claws then and there, and I would have done if I had known that Claws was about to bring us all to the brink of disaster.

But I had no inkling of that. None of us did.

We felt the static building up.

Electricity crackled in my hair.

We tore through the storm.

The *Beachcomber* shook and swayed.

The sky turned battleship grey.

We passed over an island.

I saw breaking waves.

The breaking waves went all the way to the horizon.

The sullen glowing cloud reached out for nearby mountains of vapour and dragged them into itself, building a towering castle in the heavens, spitting with energy.

We were shut in.

Something strange was happening.

The light was changing.

'Mum?'

Mum was away with the pixies. Her eyes were closed.

Without warning the islands of the Bunker Group vanished.

We smashed out of one cloud and into another. I glimpsed the sea again and was reminded of a newly ploughed field of curling, smoking furrows, their tops blowing off to form a fine mist.

This was scary.

I beckoned to Annie. We shared a window.

For one dizzying moment we were both looking down into a deep well of revolving cloud. Far down at the bottom of the well we spied churning foam.

Claws barged between us.

He wanted a look.

'Stupid storm,' he said.

Beachcomber teetered on the edge of an abyss. Annie grabbed my arm. The flying boat was all over the sky, yawing on its vertical axis, rolling on its lateral axis, and pitching on its longitudinal axis. The plane slid sideways to port and then sideways to starboard. Our stomachs churned.

For a few precious moments we flew along the top of a white cloud in bright sunshine, but then the blue-grey nimbostratus closed in again.

We began to experience a new, disconcerting motion.

I stuck out my lower lip.

Mum woke up.

'Uh-oh,' she said, putting her hands on her tummy.

'My dear,' said my father quickly.

Children are sensitive to the tones of voice used by their parents.

I knew at once that something was the matter.

Dad was on edge.

Mum was not paying any attention to the storm!

How very odd.

Parents are silly. They turn your life into one big whitewash. Your mother and father never tell you what is really going on. We little pitchers have big ears, it is true, but our ears don't really help. It is what goes on *between* our ears that suffers.

Mum and Dad knew something that I didn't.

I cast my mind back, trying to solve the enigma. My mother had spent a great deal of time in our cabin in the *Orcades*. Why?

She had put on weight. Why?

She looked like an airship!

Whatever did this mean?

My teeth chattered.

I looked at my mother with fresh eyes.

'Are you getting through to the Land Beyond?' I asked, pointedly.

It was a leading question.

Her answer might shed light not merely on something awesome in the next world but also on something in our immediate future right here in this world.

Come clean, Mum. The storm is getting worse.

I wanted to know what was really going on.

Tell me, Mum. I have a right to know.

My mother looked at me and said: '*In the walls of the halls where falls the tread of the feet of the dead to the ground, no sound: but the boom of the far waterfall like doom.*'

'*Tarantella*, by Hilaire Belloc,' I answered quickly, for this was a game we played.

Mum would recite a few lines from a poem she had recited for me in the past and then I would name the poem and the poet.

But why this poem? Why now?

And why the *last lines*?

I scratched my head.

Annie came to my rescue. Annie was wise in the ways of the world. Annie knew that grown-ups say one thing when they mean another, just like actors.

'Does it hurt awfully?' Annie asked my mother.

'Not yet,' replied Mum, and smiled back at Annie. She liked Annie. Annie grinned back at her.

I had a sudden revelation.

Annie was a *girl*.

On the ship, in the library, on our last day together, Annie had suggested that I kiss her goodbye.

'Where?' I had said.

She had pointed to her mouth. 'Here, I think,' she had said.

I had stepped forward.

I had kissed her.

She had been eating Maltesers.

She had cried after we kissed.

Being a girl was different from being a boy.

Girls knew things.

They knew that one day they might become *mothers*.

I looked from Annie to my mother, and then back at Annie. Boy, was I missing something!

So I tried reciting the first lines of the poem out loud:

Do you remember an Inn, Miranda?
Do you remember an Inn?

'It is all about Miranda,' I said.

When you haven't a clue, always say something that sounds as if you know tons more than you really do. Then, if you are lucky, the adults will assume you've cottoned on, and say something that gives everything away.

It worked, sort of. Mum treated me to a mysterious smile and said 'You may be meeting Miranda soon. Can you hear her heart beating?'

'Yes,' I said, lying through my teeth. The poem about Miranda did have a heartbeat rhythm to it.

It sounded like galloping.

But what had galloping to do with anything?

Were my parents going to buy me a pony?

I sprang to the stirrup, and Joris, and he;
I galloped, Dirck galloped, we galloped all
three…

'Miranda is in a hurry?' I ventured.

'Too much of a hurry,' said my mother, and closed her eyes.

She leaned back in her seat.

The *Beachcomber* was buffeted by several short, sharp episodes of turbulence.

Everything tipped sideways.

Dr. Bennett's carefully stacked cages tumbled.

Crash!

Crash! Crash!

A cage door flew open, releasing wild things into our cabin.

The wild things growled.

They clicked.

They had eyes on stalks.

They leaped from chair to chair.

They sailed through the air.

They were *fishes*.

In the *air*.

Why were they not dying?

Annie and I looked at one another.

Ghost Ship!

We were delighted.

Our most warped and degenerate hopes were being realized before our eyes.

We were being assailed by creatures of the deep.

Glancing, dancing, backing and advancing, snapping and clapping...

The *Beachcomber* thumped into a tropical downpour.

Bright sunlight slammed in on us. A rainbow trembled outside the window.

Ignoring the leaping wildlife, Annie and I flattened our noses to the glass.

We gaped at the storm.

The whole sky spun around us majestically. We were in a revolving amphitheater made of clouds!

Something wet hit the back of my head.

Claws in my hair!

'Nick off!' I cried, shaking my head in panic. I had a cowardly urge to dive under my seat and hide.

Annie dragged herself away from the wonderful spinning sky and eyed the strange fish running amok.

'What are they?' she asked out loud.

What indeed? We could hear them popping, gurgling and clicking away as they leaped about the passenger cabin. Were they hungry?

One of them sank its teeth into our enemy's left hand.

Claws cried out and jumped up on his chair.

'Vot is this? Fish zey belong in ze vorter.'

He shook his hand vigorously, but the tenacious fish refused to let go.

'Not all fish species live in the water,' explained Dr. B quietly, coming to his rescue.

Annie and I watched with morbid fascination as the succulent doctor removed the ravenous fish from Claws's hand.

We saw Claws's blood.

It was red, just like ours.

That was odd.

The blood of ghost cats is supposed to be green.

'*Periophthalmus argentilineatus* is an air-breathing fish,' the doctor explained as she applied iodine and a sticking plaster to Claws's wound. 'She will drown if she stays too long underwater.'

Then the doctor turned to Annie and me. 'Would you like to help me put these delightful creatures back in their cage?'

We were thrilled. We forgot all about the storm and raced around the cabin helping Dr. B recapture her leaping fishes.

There were fishes that breathed air.

How surprising!

This was turning out to be flight filled with surprises.

We did not know that the biggest surprise of all was still to come.

6: Dicey-Do

'DO YOU LIVE a very dangerous life?' asked Annie, as she put one of the escaped fishes back in its cage.

Dr. B grinned. 'Depends what you call dangerous. I collected these fishes in a mangrove-fringed mud flat near Cairns. I thought they would be clumsy out of the water and easy to lay my hands on.' She made a grab for a *Periophthalmus* that had landed on top of one of the specimen cages, but the fish hopped out of the way. 'But I was wrong. See how quick they are? A friend of mine had joined me for the collecting trip. She stood on the jetty and watched me enter the mud dressed in rubber waders that went up to my thighs. She laughed when I waded out into the oozy slime. I couldn't for the life of me think why she found me so funny.

'Are there many women scientists?' asked Annie.

'We could do with a few more. Anyway, I waded through that gooey mud trying to catch the little tykes, but they seemed to think it all a game. They would stay perfectly still until I almost had my hands on them, and then leap into a pool.'

'Just when one of them had darted down a crab-burrow and left me standing there looking stupid, I heard the worst sound in the whole world.'

'What is the worst sound in the whole world?' I asked eagerly.

Dr. B paused for a moment, remembering. 'The worst sound in the world is the sound of a hungry saltie slapping its tail.'

She clapped her hands together to make a loud bang. She grabbed one of the elusive air-breathing fishes and popped the creature back into the cage.

'Got you!' she said, and grinned at us.

'A hungry *saltie*?' asked Annie, anxious to hear more. 'What's a saltie?'

'You don't know what a saltie is? Is this your first time in Queensland?' asked Dr. B.

'This is our first time in Australia,' said Annie, and she waved her arm to show that Claws and I were as new to the country as she.

Dr. B looked the three of us over.

'The saltie I met was six feet long and covered in scales, with a wide snout. She was carrying her babies in her mouth. She spat out her young. She charged down the beach. I had invaded her territory. Territory is a serious business if you are saltie. She hit the mud with a great splat, her huge scaly tail thrashing from side to side, and she opened her mouth wide. When I saw that the teeth in her upper jaw were perfectly lined up with the teeth in her bottom jaw, I turned round and made my way back to the jetty just as fast I could wade. I could feel that saltie breathing down my neck! She nearly had me. At the last moment my friend reached down, took my hand, hauled me up onto the jetty, and I was safe.'

My friend could not stop laughing.

"You should have seen your face!" she said.

"You didn't tell me there were salties in these mud flats!"

I was put out.

"No, I did not tell you," my friend replied, patting my arm. "I know what you scientists are like. I didn't think it would be any use to warn you. When you people are after something, you don't let a little thing like a salt water crocodile stop you.""

The penny dropped.

'A saltie is a *crocodile*,' I said.

'A saltie is a crocodile that swims in the ocean,' Dr. B said, slipping another *Periophthalmus* back into its habitat box.

'Stupid crocodile,' said Claws.

'Fairly stupid, yes,' Dr. B agreed. 'Our saltwater elephants are more intelligent that our saltwater crocodiles,' she added.

My jaw dropped. Oz was filled with wonders. 'You have saltwater *elephants*?'

'Oh yes,' said Dr. B, scooping up another of the hopping fishes. 'They are not as big as the land elephants of Africa and India because they don't have to be. Our saltwater elephants grow to a length of nine feet, which is taller than me and twice as high as you. I saw my very first saltwater elephant from the deck of a research vessel. A sailor pointed her out to me in the twilight. 'A mermaid nursing her child!' he cried. He was so excited, for he had waited all his life to see a mermaid, and now at last he had spied one reclining upon a rock outcrop not far from the shore. When I told him she was not a mermaid with her child but a sea elephant with her baby, he was disappointed, but I was thrilled and ran to fetch my tape recorder. I was anxious to record the call of the sea elephant.'

'We rode on an elephant in Ceylon,' I said. 'He was called Old Boot. He made a noise like this.' I held my nose and trumpeted.

'You rode on his back? So you know how thick the legs of land elephants are. They have hold up all that weight. Saltwater elephants weigh half a ton but they have an easier time of it. Their weight is largely supported by the buoyancy of the seawater, so their limbs are thinner.'

'What did the saltwater elephant sound like?' asked Annie.

'I recorded her murmuring to her young. She made soft squawks. "Duyong, duyong," she said gently, and then again "Duyong, duyong." Her baby made no reply. Perhaps the baby had not yet learned how to speak.'

'My Dad wants to see a turtle,' I said.

'Does he? Well, he has come at just the right time of year to see turtles come ashore on Heron Island. The Loggerhead is the largest. A Loggerhead turtle can weigh up to fifteen hundred pounds. Then there is the Hawksbill, with its beak-like mouth. The Hawksbill weighs around three hundred pounds, but by far the commonest turtle on Heron Island is our sturdy Green turtle.

A Green turtle weighs about as much as the Hawksbill but the plates on its shell don't overlap. They are joined at the edges.

You'll probably see a Green turtle come ashore to lay her eggs tonight. The females are just starting at this time of year.'

'They come ashore? How?'

'Well, usually the Green turtle comes ashore under cover of darkness, after swimming for hundreds of miles to find Heron Island, the place where she was born.

She is fairly agile in the water, but once out on the sand she finds the going quite tough.

Pulling with her front flippers and heaving with her hind ones she lurches forward, stopping every few paces to have a rest because she is so tired after all her swimming.'

'Wow!' I said.

'Poor thing,' said Annie.

'Stupid turtle,' said Claws.

Dr. B rubbed her nose. 'The Green turtle leaves tracks behind in the sand, two parallel rows of flipper marks, and a dotted line left behind by her tail. Well above the tide line, she sets about building her nest. She starts digging with quick movements of her front flippers. She throws sand back to her hind flippers, and then with her *hind* flippers she kicks that same sand away to make a big heap.'

'Grab ze turtle, turn upside down, roast over fire, make soup,' said Claws.

'That can happen,' Dr. B admitted, 'but not on Heron Island where the turtles are protected.'

Claws made a face.

Annie applauded.

'Go on,' I said. 'What does the turtle do next?'

'Does she start laying?' asked Annie.

'She has to stop and have a rest from time to time. But before morning, she digs a hole big enough for her whole body to fit inside. Then she scrambles down into the hole and begins work on her egg pit.'

'Her *what*?'

'Her egg pit. She digs with her hind flippers a pit about a foot wide and about a foot and half deep.

When the egg pit is ready, she folds her hind flippers over it and lays her eggs.

The eggs are white and flexible. They are one and a third inches across. She lays these eggs at a rate of about four or five a minute.

The more she lays, the faster the eggs come out. When she has laid one hundred and twenty eggs, she fills in her egg pit with sand to cover up her eggs and keep them safe.

She uses both her front and hind flippers to push the heaped sand back into the nest. Finally the turtle levels everything off. She makes the sand smooth so that nobody will know where she has laid her eggs.

Only when she has finished tidying up the beach does she make her way back to the water, dragging her tail behind her. This huge endeavor, perhaps the most important in her life, can take her up to seven hours.

When she is done, sliding back down the beach to the sea is not so hard. She slips into the ocean where her husband has been waiting anxiously for her all night long.'

'Where do she and her husband swim off to?' I wondered aloud.

'That is good question,' said Dr. B. 'Nobody knows.'

'It must be fun being a scientist,' said Annie.

'It is the best job in the world. There! I think that is the last of our hopping fishes safely back in captivity. I thank you for your help,' said Dr. B.

She closed the cage door with a snap.

We heard a gasp. It came from our cabin.

Dr. B straightened up. She cocked her head. 'What was that?'

Dad put his head around the corner. 'Doctor, I hate to trouble you but may I have a quick word? It's my wife.'

Dad and Dr. B left in a hurry, knocking another cage askew on the way. Something inside the cage wriggled and spluttered. Annie made a run for our cabin.

I was left alone with Claws. I wanted to see what was wrong with Mum but Claws would not let me go. He pushed me behind the Electric Eel enclosure. 'Your Mooter die soon,' he said.

'She's not going to die,' I told him. 'Stop pushing!'

'Baby stuck inside. Baby die. Mooter die.'

'You're a *liar*. I *hate* you. If you say that again, I'll give you an *axe kick*.'

'Mooter die,' said Claws, and shoved me again, daring me to try.

'Kiai!' I gave Claws the axe kick. One good kick should finish him off. My book said so.

Claws saw my axe kick coming and ducked to one side.

My foot hit his shoulder.

Claws countered with a lunge punch.

I flew through the air.

I ended up jammed in a gap between the archerfish tank and the robber crab cage.

I was stunned.

I could not breathe.

I was undone.

Claws had read the same book.

I was trying hard to gulp in air but nothing was happening.

I might never breathe again.

My combat manual had warned me about the dangers of the axe kick.

You leave your body exposed.

I tried once again to fill my lungs.

Nothing happened.

It was no good.

I was dead.

I could see Claws closing in for the kill.

I made one last tremendous effort.

I gasped.

I could breathe again!

I felt air flood back into my lungs.

I pulled myself together in a hurry.

Maybe Claws did not know how to do the chicken-head.

I swung myself around the tank and sat on him.

I reached for his neck.

Claws would not allow this.

Claws employed a sliding elbow block!

Scissor punch!

Hook kick!

Oof!

Rays undulated.

An anglerfish dangled a lure.

Claws pinned me down. He whispered in my ear. I did not want to hear what Claws had to say. I challenged him.

'I don't want to hear about the horrible things that had happened in the camp, Claws!'

'They pull out teeth,' said Claws.

I nearly fainted. 'That's not true. They wouldn't.'

It *was* true. I could tell by his voice.

They pulled out teeth.

What other horrid things did they do?

I didn't want to know.

Claws told me.

He made me listen.

They had done *what?*

I wanted to throw up.

I wrenched myself away.

I was furious with Claws for telling me of the cruelties he had witnessed and angry with myself for listening.

I was so angry I could hardly speak.

The world couldn't be like that.

I would not *let* the world be like that.

Mum cried out in pain.

I ran to see what was the matter.

7: Hoosh

MUM looked sweaty and hot. She barely looked at me.

I bit my tongue.

She screwed up her face, and trembled.

I could not bear it.

What did dead people sound like anyway?

'Maybe Hitler is trying to reach you,' I suggested helpfully, wiping fish slime off my hands onto the Barrier Reef Airways upholstery.

Mum moved her head slowly from side to side.

It was not Hitler trying to get through.

Good.

I had had quite enough of Hitler.

I tried to imagine who else might be calling from the Farther Shore.

Mum's parents had shared a flat in York Place in Edinburgh. Both had been artists.

Perhaps they were anxious to hear how their woodblocks were selling.

No.

I was missing something. I tried to put the pieces of the puzzle together: the poem about Miranda and the story about a fish named M.

It was a grown-up conspiracy.

'Dr. B,' gasped Mum in a gap between two vigorous transmissions from Beyond the Veil.

The marine biologist grinned.

'Bottle-nosed dolphins gestate for twelve months,' she said, 'and afterwards they nurse for eighteen months.'

Mum looked sideways at Claws, Annie and me.

Dad whispered in Dr. B's ear.

I sighed.

I knew what was coming.

We were kids.

We weren't supposed to know what was going on.

When grown-ups start using long words like 'gestate' you *know* you are in trouble.

Dr. B listened carefully to what my Dad had to say.

'Perhaps it would be for the best,' she agreed, and strode up the aisle to the cockpit.

She returned in a matter of minutes with the captain in tow.

'How's our artist?' the captain asked, beaming down at me.

Uh-oh.

It was kidnapping time. I could tell.

I grew red in the face. It was the fish slime! I had wiped my hands on a Barrier Reef Airways seat cover! The captain was here to punish me. He would take me forward and remove my teeth.

'I'm all right,' I said between my teeth, keeping my mouth as tightly closed as possible.

'In bonzer weather like this,' the captain went on blithely, 'we invite nippers up front. Want to give it a crack?

It was all a ruse. Whatever nippers were, I was sure they would hurt. I had an inspiration. There might be safety in numbers.

'Yes, please.' I nudged Annie. 'Come on. Let's go see where they fly the plane.'

'I kom,' said Claws.

Annie and I looked daggers at Claws.

Serve him right if he came with us to the cockpit.

'Say goodbye to your teeth, Claws,' I said under my breath.

Claws overheard me.

His cheeks went pale. He started to shake.

His eyes darted this way and that, seeking some way to escape.

But there was nowhere to go. We were on a plane.

I held my breath.

I considered taking desperate measures.

Biggles killed people every day. He downed dozens of red Albatrosses. His Sopwith Camel had machine guns synchronized to fire *through* his propeller.

If only I were Biggles!

But I was just Anthony Barton.

I breathed out.

'Come with us then,' I said to Claws. 'Come with us to the flight deck if you must.'

Filled with dread, the three of us followed the captain.

We were very, very scared.

Mum wanted us out of the way.

I took a quick look over my shoulder to have one last look at my mother while I still had my teeth.

The Dead were growing more persistent.

Mum was gasping.

Dr. B was rearranging the seats to make a bed for her.

Dad was talking about hot water and towels.

He wanted to take a bath? In a flying boat?

That couldn't be it.

Why was Dad going on about hot water and towels, then? I didn't think he'd have much luck. There was nowhere to heat water in the *Beachcomber*, and the only towel I had seen had been the one beside the washbasin in the dunny with the walking stick.

We followed the captain between the stacks of cages housing Dr. B.'s menagerie.

'They are going to pull out our teeth,' I whispered to Annie.

Annie did Dorothy confronts the Scarecrow.

'What for?' she asked.

I was uncertain how to answer.

We were to be treated like the prisoners in a concentration camp, but I dared not tell her that we were being punished because I had wiped fish slime off my hands onto a Barrier Reef Airways seat cover.

I decided to improvise.

Why did bad things happen?

Why did bad people exist?

I hadn't a clue.

I thought hard.

I had to give Annie and Claws a plausible explanation for the unspeakable horrors awaiting us in the cockpit.

'All children who come to Oz have their teeth out. When the pilots have removed our teeth, we shall be given a golden cap.'

'Vot is dis?' asked Claws. 'Golden cap?'

'You put the golden cap on your head and say the secret formula to summon the Winged Monkeys. It is hard to say when you have no teeth, so the monkeys may not come.'

Claws looked nervous. He looked around him at the stacked crates filled with wild creatures. 'Monkeys with Vings?'

'We may call the Winged Monkeys to do our bidding three times. On each occasion we must tell the monkeys what to do and then the monkeys will do *exactly* what we tell them.'

Dr. B had left her rubber gloves on top of the crate containing the electric eel from Brazil.

Claws snatched up the gloves.

He put them on.

'Claws! Stop! What are you doing? She said it was dangerous!'

Claws lifted something long and squirming from the bright yellow cage plastered with warning labels.

'Not pull teeth,' he said. 'Zap with eel.'

Annie and I gasped.

'Claws, put that thing back in its tank at once! We're in enough trouble already.'

Annie and I knew full well what Claws had just pulled out of the tank.

Dr. B had demonstrated the shocking power of that electric eel to us after we had helped her round up her hopping fishes.

Dr. B had begun by inviting us to peer into the murky water of the eel's tank. 'Notice the wavy motion of the long ventral fin,' she had said.

'*Electrophorus electricus* is not really an eel,' she had gone on to say. '*Electrophorus* is another example of an air-breathing fish. She's completely blind. She does not need eyes because she forms a picture of the world around her by sending out pulses of energy into her surroundings and then detecting the echoes that bounce back.'

'Like sonar in a submarine?' I had chipped in.

'Something like that,' Dr. B had agreed. 'But now we come to the interesting part,' she had said, pulling on her rubber gloves and waggling her fingers. 'The electric eel's body contains two hundred and fifty thousand electric cells. Each cell generates one tenth of a volt. The cells are arranged in series like the batteries in a torch. The fish can turn on all of the cells at once just by thinking. Her electric cells are attached to one another. Would you care to take part in a small experiment?'

Dr. B had picked up two slender aluminum electrodes and had invited Annie and Claws to hold them tightly.

We had shrunk away from the doctor, thinking her quite mad.

'Don't worry,' she had said. 'So long as the three of you hold hands then each of you will receive only one third of the five hundred volt shock.'

I had grasped Annie's hand in my right hand and Claws's hand in my left, and Dr. B had placed an electrode in Annie's right hand and another electrode in Claws's left hand.

Then she had lifted with her gloved hands a squirming five feet long electric fish from the tank and placed the grey creature on the top of a crate.

'Ready?'

Dr. B had applied the leads from the electrodes to the body of the 'eel' in two places about a foot apart.

I had felt a sudden tug of electric energy course through me. My hair had stood on end. Annie and Claws had felt the same jolt of energy. We had dropped the electrodes in a hurry.

'That was just a low voltage shock,' Dr. B had explained. 'Were I to apply the leads to points *four feet apart* on the body of the animal then you would all have ended up lying on the floor, stunned. That is how the *Electrophorus electricus* knocks out the fishes upon which she feeds. First she shocks them out of their minds. Then she eats them.'

That had been earlier. Now it was Claws who was shocking Annie and me out of our minds.

'Somebody try pull teeth, I zap them with eel,' said Claws, holding up the wriggling horror.

'Put it back, Claws!' I said angrily. I become angry when I am frightened. 'Put it back right now!'

Claws shook his head and held the wriggling specimen of *Electrophorus electricus* behind his back and out of our reach.

'Come along,' said the captain patiently, looking over his shoulder.

Then the captain led the three of us onto the flight deck, never suspecting for a moment what Claws was bringing with him.

8: Cockup

THE CAPTAIN led the three of us onto the flight deck of the Boeing PB2B-2R Catalina. As soon as we had all entered the cockpit, the captain closed and locked the door, effectively shutting us off from my mother's cries and from the rapidly developing crisis in the passenger area.

Yes, he locked the door.

That made it as clear as day for me.

It was teeth time.

We three children were being removed from whatever was going on in the passenger cabin. The grown-ups wanted us out of the way. My Mum did not want me or Annie or Claws running back to help. Mum had some business to attend to. But what kind of business?

I suspected that it had something to do with Miranda and the hip! hop! hap! of the clap of the hands to the swirl and the twirl of the girl.

But my mind was in something of a whirl.

Mum knew I'd be safe inside in the cockpit having my teeth removed. Perhaps a new set of teeth would grow in afterwards? Perhaps this wonderful amazing cockpit would serve as a distraction?

I looked about me in awe.

We had been exiled to a land of wonders. While sketching the plane earlier I had been surprised to find the cockpit of the Catalina forward of the wings and of the twin engines, and had wondered if that gave the pilots a clear view.

It did.

The vista was smashing.

From this inner sanctum of the pilots we could see for miles and miles.

A tremendous array of instruments, dials, knobs and switches lay before me.

I was in heaven.

During my five-week voyage to Oz I had read my Biggles books curled up in my bunk, and in *The Camels are Coming* and *Biggles Goes to War* I had imagined myself seated in a cockpit of my own plane and reaching for the throttle.

In my mind's eye I had seen the rim of the sun, glowing like molten metal, show above the horizon, and I had dreamed that I felt the dawn wind make my aircraft rise and fall like a ship riding an ocean.

I had seemed to hear the defiant roar of my engine drop to a deep-throated growl as my aircraft's sleek nose had tilted downwards. I had longed to be a pilot like Biggles!

And now, for the first time in my life, I was up in the sky in a true aircraft, and standing on a working flight deck.

There were windows on all sides and overhead.

The spectacle took my breath away. The heavens were alive! Glowing white clouds were coming toward us. We were walled in on either hand by mountains of cumulonimbus. I spied a flock of rosy-headed galahs.

'Holy dooley!' I said. There was a burst of static and a faraway voice spoke from the copilot's headset.

'Roger, Barrier Reef Victor. Confirm you carrying information Echo...maintain one three thousand...call fifteen minutes west of Heron Island – Over.'

'BRV maintaining one three thousand feet...will call fifteen minutes west of Heron Island on one two six decimal seven – Over.'

'Heron Island Radio...This is Barrier Reef Victor...Fifteen minutes west of Heron Island at four seven...requesting further clearance.'

'ATC clears BRV to descend immediately, report leaving one two thousand five hundred. Traffic westbound Aero Commander maintaining eight thousand estimating Heron Island at five six...'

'BRV is cleared to descend immediately – Report leaving one two thousand five hundred. Check the traffic as westbound Aero Commander at Eight Thousand. Over.'

'Heron Island Radio... BRV leaving one two thousand five hundred. Requesting latest Heron Island weather and altimeter.'

'BRV check you leaving one two thousand five hundred at five zero...latest Heron Island weather – One thousand scattered... Altimeter two niner zero three...cleared to join circuit downwind – wind two seven zero at one five. Start squawk one two hundred. Call when turning final. Over.'

'Are those reefs?' Annie asked, pressing her cheek to the side window.

I ran to join her, anxious to see for myself.

What a sight!

In the dim light of the storm a chain of atolls shone in sweeping curves of turquoise and emerald. The atolls were divided from the deep ultramarine blue of the deeps by thin white lines of breaking waves.

'That's where the banana benders live,' said the captain cheerfully. 'That's Fairfax Island down there and Hoskyn coming up on the horizon. He turned to me. 'Want to feel how a flying boat handles, Anthony?' he asked, and gestured to the empty left-hand seat.

Hardly daring to believe my good fortune, I lost no time in scrambling into the captain's seat of *Beachcomber*.

'Keep your airspeed above one sixty.'

For the first time in my life I was at the controls of an aircraft! Of course the copilot was beside me in the right seat, so I was pretty sure that he was the one really flying the plane, and I was just a passenger. But all the same, it felt jolly good, even if it was only pretending.

I noticed that the copilot was using both his hands *and his feet* to fly the flying boat. His hands were grasping a stick shaped like the bottom half of the driving wheel of a car, while his feet were resting on pedals. I was not sure what the pedals were for. The captain's seat on which I was perched had a similar half steering wheel and similar pedals. I held onto the steering column as if my life depended on it.

The metal felt cold.

I could sense the plane vibrating!

'Wizard!' I said.

I tried moving the control column gently. I wondered what would happen if both the copilot and I tried to fly the plane at the same time.

In between the two pilots' seats were mounted throttle and mix levers that could be moved forward or backward in slots. They resembled the gear levers in cars. One had a red knob like a cricket ball. Another had a green knob. I wondered what the knobbed levers were for. I was eager to move one just to see what happened, but restrained myself.

The control panel before me had many of the instruments I recalled reading about in my Biggles books. I spotted the Air Speed Indicator, the Vertical Speed Indicator, the Artificial Horizon, and the Turn and Bank Indicator. In the middle of the panel were two tachometers measuring the RPMs for each engine. Close to me was the Altimeter. The Gyro Compass was overhead. Where was the Magnetic Compass? Down at the bottom was an ammeter for the onboard electrical systems.

In the middle of the control panel between the two pilots, I found two fuel gauges. It would be necessary to turn on the auxiliary fuel pumps for landing.

If I stretched out my legs I could just reach the pedals by sitting on the very edge of the seat and pointing my toes.

Through my feet I could feel the aircraft shaking.

I was flying a plane!

But it couldn't really be true, could it? They wouldn't be so foolish as to let a child fly a plane. Unless, I thought hopefully, they were idiots? Oh please, let them be idiots.

'Am I really flying *The Beachcomber*?' I asked hopefully.

The captain shot a look at Frank Kelly and raised an eyebrow.

Frank took his hands from the controls and held them up in the air!

'Fair dinkum,' he said, and grinned at me.

'I'll be stuffed!' I said.

For a few desperate and wonderful moments I flew the plane all by myself.

I felt fairly safe doing so, knowing that two reliable pilots were standing by to take over the moment I made a mistake, but it was a thrill.

My breath came quickly. My heart raced.

All of this attention on me had infuriated Claws. He was angry that it was *me* the captain had invited to fly the plane and not *him*. He was convinced we were all about to have our teeth extracted. So he held up the writhing *Electrophorus electricus* he had snatched from Dr. Bennett's collection.

'Look vot I haf!' he said, as bold as brass.

He was sure his threat would cow the evil pilots into submission. The moment they saw the electric fish they would know their number was up. We would be released from captivity and allowed to return to the passenger cabin.

'Be careful!' I said, looking at him over my shoulder and quite forgetting that I was flying *Beachcomber*. 'That's a dangerous animal, Claws. Remember how big a shock it gave us. Don't let it touch anything.'

The electric fish writhed in Claws's rubber-gloved hands.

I suppose the wretched beast was angry. It was trying to escape from Claws. I could not blame it for that. Like the air-breathing fishes that had growled and clicked their way about the cabin, leaping from seat to seat, this electric fish did not mind being out of the water at all, but perhaps it wanted to revenge itself on this foolish boy who had kicked in its cage and hauled it out. Whatever its motive may have been, the electric fish decided that this was an emergency and that it was time to deploy its most potent weapon.

There was a sound like frying bacon.

Claws's hair stood on end!

'Yucky snake!' cried Claws and flung the sizzling creature from him.

By sheer chance the electric fish landed in the copilot's lap.

There was second sizzle. Dr. B had taught us that *Electrophorus electricus* recharges itself in less than one thousandth of a second.

The copilot shook from head to toe. He leaped to his feet, twitching. He staggered from his chair. His eyes rolled up into his head. He collapsed. His headgear fell off.

'Frank?' said the captain, alarmed. He hurried to loosen the collar of his copilot.

There was a third sputtering frizzle and the captain fell to his knees, toppled over sideways, thrashed about for a while and then lay there on his back on the cockpit floor, his eyes wide open, staring at nothing.

Claws panicked. He ran to the cabin door, and rattled the handle.

'Zey take out our teeth!' he shouted.

Nothing happened. Nobody heard him. Nobody came.

'Dad!' I shouted.

'Help!' screamed Annie.

But the roar of the engines drowned our cries.

Annie and I stared at one another wide-eyed.

This wasn't Ghost Ship.

This was real.

We were locked in the cockpit of a flying boat with a dangerous electric fish, two senseless pilots, and our sworn enemy.

'Stupid snake!' Claws sat down with his back to the locked door. He began to cry.

The air on the flight deck smelled of ozone.

Annie and I looked down at the pilots.

Both lay stretched out on the deck. Both had their eyes wide open.

Both were unconscious. Or dead. It was beyond our powers to tell which. It crossed my mind that if the pilots were indeed dead, they might get in touch with Mum from the Land

Beyond. But then Mum had troubles enough of her own right now.

And if the two pilots were still alive, they were showing no signs of coming round any time soon.

Boy, that electric fish had packed a wallop! Where was that fish? Where had it gone? I could not see it. Oh, boy!

This was way beyond Holy Dooley.

I took a deep breath.

Why have we not crashed?

The answer came to me like a thunderbolt.

Because I am flying the plane.

The electric fish was by my feet! It wriggled into a gap between the wainscot and the control console and vanished from sight.

I wished the fish well. I hoped it would not chew on any electric wires in there.

'Captain? Wake up!' said Annie desperately. 'Mr. Kelly?'

'Don't touch either of them,' I said. 'Their bodies may still be charged.'

'I have to,' she said, and she shook the captain by his shoulders.

No response.

She shook the copilot by his shoulders.

Nothing.

9: Sparks

'BOTH PILOTS!' she said, shocked.

She swooned. Wow! You should have seen Annie swoon!

She was smashing. First she made herself go weak at the knees, and then she rolled her eyes.

What a performance!

I had seen Rita Heyworth swoon once, in a film, so I knew a good swoon when I saw one. Swooning was a Hollywood specialty. They had an entire class devoted to swooning at the Academy of Motion Picture Arts and Sciences.

I said in my deepest voice 'No worries, Annie. Everything is going to be fine. I'm flying the plane.'

I would have brushed an imaginary tear from my cheek while saying this to let the audience know I was fibbing, but dared not let go of the steering column. Besides, there was no audience.

There was just me.

Lonely.

In command.

'Annie?'

No answer.

'*Annie!*'

Annie grinned and sat up. 'You really know how to fly a plane?'

'Of course not.'

What would Biggles do next?

I tried to pull myself together.

No more mucking about.

My own knees were starting to feel a bit weak.

This swooning business was catching.

I told myself sternly I had command of *Beachcomber*.

I thought of the twenty-two passengers and crew, and knew what I had to do. I had to fly the plane to Heron Island and land it somehow.

To pilot a flying boat I would need help. Annie was my best friend. She might want to assist me. 'Annie, I'm flying the plane. I need you to put on the copilot's headgear, sit in the right hand seat, and help me.'

The copilot's headgear was made of soft leather. It lay on the deck. Annie put it on her head. Flaps covered her ears.

She hopped up onto the seat vacated by the copilot. She sat there swinging her legs and staring at all the dials and switches. 'This is batty,' she said. 'What do I do?'

'Do you remember when the copilot operated the radio?

'Yes.'

'We need to talk to someone on the ground. Someone who knows how to fly a Catalina.'

'I saw the copilot turn this knob. It says TRANSMITTER.'

'Try it.'

I heard voices crackle in Annie's helmet. 'Turn right heading zero six zero, descend and maintain five thousand, slow to two two zero knots. Victor-How-Baker-Roger-Able, contact Heron Island one-one-eight-point-seven.'

'That's us!' I said, excitedly, doing my best to keep the plane flying straight and level and talk at the same time.

I looked straight ahead. Churning clouds came slowly towards me and then rushed past. Then I noticed with horror that everything, the entire sky, was sagging to the right!

Oh, no! Heaven help us!

What did I have to do to keep the machine flying straight and level?

I tried easing back on the control column to pitch the nose up. Now I could see more blue sky. That did not seem to help much. We were still sagging to the right. I had a sinking feeling in my tummy. Pulling the stick back had made matters worse. I tried moving the control column a little to the left, and gave a sigh of relief when the sky straightened out. Phew! We were not sagging anymore!

I was getting the hang of things.

I could steer, sort of.

Gingerly I pushed the control column forwards. Better. Now I could see the cobalt and turquoise blues of Hoskyn Island.

Slowly at first and then faster and faster the nose of the plane dipped downward.

Oh, no!

The *Beachcomber* was going into a dive.

We were plunging downwards. We were rocketing towards a coral atoll.

We were going to crash. Why? What had I done wrong?

Annie bit her lip. She did not to scream.

Good for Annie.

'Stupid airplane,' said Claws, hauling himself to his feet. He grabbed the edge of the control panel, his tears forgotten.

I watched the airspeed indicator: one eighty five, one ninety, one ninety-five, two hundred...

I felt helpless.

Right in front of me in the middle of my side of the control panel was an instrument with a white thing in the middle and two white 'wings' on either side to represent the plane in relation to the horizon. The white wing on the left had tilted downward, while the white wing on the right had risen up, and both were staying that way.

I cast about in my mind. I had read about a crisis something like this in *Biggles Learns to Fly*. My machine was in a dive. What had Biggles had done to pull out of a dive? I racked my brains trying to recall the words in the book.

The one hundred foot hand on the altimeter was going backwards so fast I could hear it ticking, while the one thousand foot hand was moving less quickly, but it was speeding up.

Biggles had hauled the joystick towards his chest to save himself. That was what he had done.

Would the same trick work for the *Beachcomber*?

I hauled back on the control column with all my might. 'Come on, *Beachcomber!* Up, you brute!' I shouted.

Talk about batty.

I had gone completely nuts.

We were all about to die.

The bright waters of the Hoskyn atoll were so close I spied shadowy shoals of fishes flashing their silver scales in the half-light. The screw pines were thrashing about in the storm, their stilt-like roots hanging on for dear life.

'*Beachcomber*! Stop mucking around!'

Slowly, so slowly, like the elephant we had ridden in Ceylon, the flying boat responded to my hauling back on the stick.

The altimeter needles slowed, came to a stop, and then began to wind back up as we laboriously regained height. Thank heavens! We were pulling out of our dive.

I wiped my brow.

We were climbing!

Then I remembered the captain's advice.

'Watch the airspeed, Annie. Tell me if it goes below one six zero.'

As the flying boat climbed, bearing the weight of her cargo, her passengers, and my parents back up into the sky, I began to feel a growing sluggishness about her.

I blew a raspberry.

'Holy-dooley!' I said.

The flying boat was *slowing*.

Annie squeaked. 'The airspeed. It's at ninety! It's going down! Eighty-five, eighty…'

'Pigs bum,' I swore.

My most terrible oath.

The entire flight deck tilted.

'We are going to stall.'

A cup slid off the navigation console and smashed to pieces.

I racked my brains. Biggles had told his cousin Algy about stalls. 'Keep your head,' he had said. *Easier said than done.* 'Use your brain,' he had said. *Not much left of my brain.* My teacher at Grimwade House had thrown a shoe at my head every time I had made a mistake. The more shoes he had thrown, the more mistakes I had made. *I probably have permanent brain damage.* I'd like to see my teacher try to fly a Catalina.

'If she spins, you're done for,' Biggles had said.

Think!

Which way was *The Beachcomber* stalling? She was stalling to the *right*.

So…

Stick forward and hard opposite rudder. I pushed the control yoke forwards as far as it would go. I extended my leg, found a pedal, and did my best to push it.

Annie grew excited. 'We're speeding up again!'

Actually, we were falling out of the sky. Was I applying opposite rudder? I wasn't sure.

I could hardly reach the pedals with my feet and to make matters even more confusing *The Beachcomber* was a *flying boat*. The pedal I was pushing might be for taxiing in the water for all I knew.

I took a gamble. I moved the control column to the left.

'The sea!' cried Annie. 'I can see the waves!'

I leveled off. Wahoo! I was flying by the seat of my pants. I was Biggles. I was crabbing along.

'Hang on!' I said.

I saw silver gulls. I saw spume from the tops of the waves splatter across the windscreen. Swells rose and fell inches beneath us. We tore through the air skimming immense, storm-tossed seas. We were alive.

Just.

The Beachcomber was still flying.

We were skimming along just above the waves.

Not good.

Very tenderly this time I pulled the control stick back towards me, and waited patiently for the flying boat to respond.

Gently, gently. *Easy does it*, I said to myself. *No more stalling. A slow, steady climb this time.*

The flying boat responded and began yet another laborious ascent, fighting the storm.

The sea and the seabirds dropped away beneath us.

This time Annie and I watched the instruments like hawks, waiting for the next alarming thing to happen.

We had been lucky so far.

But how long was our luck going to last?

We were in level flight.

'I need someone on the ground to teach me how to fly,' I reminded Annie. 'Can you work the radio?'

'There is a knob with four positions: OFF, VOICE, CW and MCW.'

'Try them all.'

'Another knob, labelled CHANNEL. There are eleven numbers. The knob is pointing to position number 1.'

'Try everything.'

Click.

Click.

'We have a red light.'

'Say something. Anything.'

Annie pulled herself together. 'Mayday, mayday, mayday,' she said. 'Come in, Heron island. This is Annie.'

10: Mayday

'HERON ISLAND RADIO... What's happened to Frank?' said a surprised voice from the copilot's headset.

Annie lost no time in explaining. 'The copilot was zapped by an electric eel. The captain went to help him and got zapped too. Anthony and me are flying the plane. Talk us down, Heron Island.'

'I'll be stuffed. How old are you, Annie?'

'I'm ten. Anthony is nine.'

'Fair dinkum?'

'Fair dinkum.'

'Look, kids. Is there anyone, anyone at all, on board know how to fly?'

'We're locked in the cockpit. We can't get out, they can't get in, and nobody in the passenger cabin can hear us because Anthony's Mum is having a baby.'

The flying boat gave a lurch.

'My Mum is having a *baby*?'

My life had just chucked a U-e.

You talk to the Dead and they give you a baby!

That was the big grown-up secret! Now it all made sense: Tarantella, Miranda, the Ghost Ship...

The high peaks hoar and the torrent at the door! It was all part of an age-old story, and I was just too busy piloting right now to grasp that story fully, but no doubt I would fathom it soon, if only I could keep this flying boat in the air and find Heron Island.

I heard cries of pain from the cabin. It was Mum! It had to be. Dear heavens! What were the Dead doing to her?

I looked at Annie. I was desperate.

'Tell Heron Island we'll call them back,' I said.

'We'll call you back, Heron Island,' said Annie.

'What could make my Mum scream like that?'

'The woman cries out, somebody dabs her forehead to keep the sweat out of her eyes, and then other people tell her to push.'

'And then?' I asked, bewildered.

Annie shrugged. 'Quick dissolve to the joyful mother being handed a baby.'

I whistled.

What a sell-out.

Grown-ups!

They never tell you the whole story.

I was trying my best to hold the control

column as steady as possible but storm gusts were buffeting the *Beachcomber*.

I stared down at my feet. 'Annie, what do you think the pedals are for?'

'Which do you want most? A brother? Or a sister?'

'A brother. But Mum wants me to have a sister. She plans to call her Miranda. Don't worry. Babies don't happen in planes. Babies happen in hospitals. Let's find Heron Island. All the islands look the same from up here. Get back on the horn. Tell them we just passed over Hoskyn. Ask them what course we should steer for Heron Island. Tell them we need to know what the island looks like from up in the air.'

Annie fiddled with the radio knobs.

The red light came on again.

She blew into the microphone.

'It's me again, Heron Island,' said Annie brightly. 'We just passed over Hoskyn Island. What course please?'

'Barrier Reef Victor, this is Heron Island. Affirmative your request for immediate DF steer for Heron Island. Steer 315 degrees. You will find the gyro compass indicator in front of you at the ten o'clock position.

Start a rate one turn changing your course to three one five degrees. Commence your rollout at three one ten degrees, and maintain level flight. It is high tide. Land in the lagoon, Barrier Reef Victor.'

'Thank you, Heron Island. We see the Remote Compass Indicator. How do we change course, Heron Island?'

'Bank to the left twenty degrees, and the aircraft will turn to the left. Cease banking and resume level flight when your Remote Compass Indicator says three-one-five.'

'We hear you, Heron Island. Banking now.'

I moved the yoke carefully.

'Come *on*, you beauty,' I said under my breath.

'The Remote Compass Indicator is changing. We see three-one-five. We are returning to straight and level flight.'

'Good on you. How's your airspeed?'

'Airspeed reads one eight oh,' I said.

'One eight oh miles per hour, Heron Island,' said Annie.

There was a sound of deep-fat frying and a puff of smoke drifted up from the control console.

The hissing of the radio stopped.

No more radio!

Annie and I looked at one another in horror.

'Get them back,' I said tersely.

I had to have help from the ground. I needed to hear that comforting voice.

I did not know where to land. I did not know how to land.

'Come in, Heron Island,' said Annie. 'This is Victor-How-Baker-Roger-Able. Say again, Heron Island.'

No answer.

'Try the other channels.'

Annie tried the other channels.

'I can't hear a thing,' Annie went on. 'The eel has fried the radio.'

'It may not be the eel. It may be the storm. Keep trying. Claws, go the navigation station. Find a map of the Capricorn and Bunker Islands. Hurry.'

'Vait. Vun moment. Ja, ja. I haf found ze map. From Hoskyn Island, Heron Island bears three one zero, where north is three sixty degrees. Alter course. Head three one zero.'

'But the voice said three-one-five.'

Was Claws trying to kill us?

Could I trust him?

'Allow for headwind. Big storm.'

'Three one zero, then.'

I moved the control column to my right and felt the flying boat respond.

I leveled off again, headed in a slightly more northerly direction.'

'Listen to me, Claws. We need to how to identify Heron Island from the air.'

Claws squinted at the map.

'Say here Heron Island scuttle big ship, *Protector*, make breakwater.'

'Good. Is the wreck big enough to be seen from the air?'

'*Ja.* Offshore by wharf.'

'Estimated time of arrival?'

'Airspeed, vun eight zero. Distance from Hoskyn to Heron, three six mile. ETA eleven minutes, captain.'

So Claws was good at mathematics.

His teacher hadn't thrown any shoes at *him*.

'Keep your eyes peeled. Look for an island with a wrecked ship.'

Claws had called me 'captain.'

The rat bag!

Maybe there was hope for him yet.

It was time to begin our descent.

I had a sinking feeling.

I eased the control yoke forward. Our airspeed began to increase as we headed down through the clouds.

The clouds parted.

I saw Heron Island in the distance.

There was no mistaking the wreck of the HMAS Protector.

But what was a lagoon?

I was not sure.

On what stretch of water were we supposed to land?

'Give me a landing check list, please, Claws.'

Claws dug out the pilot's manual.

He thumbed through the pages.

'Floats down. Propellers set to fine pitch, indicating 2450 rpm.'

'Annie, see if you can adjust the propellers. What about the fuel?'

'Rich,' said Claws. 'Close cowl flaps.'

'I've done the propellers and the fuel mix but I don't know how to close the cowl flaps or put the floats down,' said Annie. 'What are the cowl flaps anyway?'

'No idea. Forget them. I'm throttling back to 1000 RPM. We're going down. Here we go.'

'Prop set for landing,' said Claws.

'Annie?'

Holy-dooley! We are coming in over the trees.

We're going so fast. We're not going to pull this off!

'After hit vater, stop engines. Mixture control to idle cut off position.'

'Thanks, Claws. You're my hero. When this all over, I'll kill you.'

I throttled back.

I can do this. I have to.

'Hold on tight, Annie. You, too, Claws.'

Hang on everyone!

Pisonia trees flashed by past just under our wings. A flock of startled black noddies took to the air.

Bright blue water rushed towards us.

11: C for Charlie

I FELT A HAND on my shoulder.

'I can take her from here, Anthony,' said the captain of the *Beachcomber*.

The captain was back on his feet! The electric fish from Brazil had not killed him!

But had he recovered in time to save us?

'She's all yours,' I said hastily, and scrambled out of the captain's seat.

The captain took my place.

'When the waves are this high we like to ease her down. I'll show you.'

The captain moved the control yoke forward, pulled it back, and to my astonishment *The Beachcomber* reared up like a frightened horse and then alighted on the back of a storm-tossed wave as light as a feather.

With her hull back in the water, the *Beachcomber* slewed to the left, slewed to the right, recovered herself, and then rose up out of the water like a diving bird surfacing.

The captain steered the flying boat to her mooring.

The far side of the lagoon was bright with a blaze of wild poinsettia.

We were down.

In one piece.

The Beachcomber lost way and bobbed about in the shallows where the water was calmer.

I was tickled pink.

We were safe.

We were still alive.

'You beaut!' I whispered, patting the console. It is all right to talk to your kite. Biggles does it all the time.

We had arrived at Heron Island.

The captain turned to me. 'Bonzer show, Anthony! You too, Annie! And you too, Klaus! If you look over there you'll see our launch coming hell for leather. Somebody must have told them something was up.'

I grinned at Annie.

Annie grinned back at me. 'Wipe the sweat from your brow with the back of your hand,' she whispered.

'Like this?'

'Say "We couldn't have done it without Claws!" Say it!'

'We couldn't have done it without Claws!'

I wiped an imaginary tear from my cheek.

Somebody groaned.

It was the copilot. He was coming round. He climbed to his feet. He looked groggy.

'What happened?' he asked.

The captain grinned. 'Somebody dropped an eel in your budgy smugglers.'

The deck tilted. 'I'm zonked,' said the copilot, grabbing for the edge of the console. He peered disbelievingly out of the window. His jaw dropped. 'We've landed. We're at Heron.' Then he frowned at Annie as if seeing her for the first time. What was this slip of a girl doing sitting in his chair?

'An eel called *Electrophorus* knocked you both out,' Annie explained. 'So we flew the plane for you.'

'You what?'

'Anthony steered. I worked the radio. I borrowed your helmet. I hope you don't mind.' She handed the leather cap back to him.

The copilot stared at Annie and then at the captain. He looked down at his leather headset.

'That's about it,' said the captain, closing down his station. 'These ankle biters hijacked our flying boat. They saved the *Beachcomber*. You hear what I'm saying, Frank? Take over. I'm going back to count our passengers. These bright young people just saved our airline. Without them, we wouldn't *have* an airline.'

'But you have two other planes in your fleet,' I reminded him. 'The *Buccaneer* and the *Bermuda*. It says so in your brochure.'

'Don't believe everything you read in brochures, cobber. We use the *Buccaneer* and the *Bermuda* strictly for spare parts.'

Kelly shook his fingers as if trying to shake the electricity out of them. 'How did that creature get aboard?'

'Must have been one of Isobel's,' said the captain.

'It wriggled in here,' I said and pointed to the gap between edge of the control console and the panel. I think it shorted the radio.'

The captain bent down for a closer look. 'No eel in there now. Must have baled out. Back in the water, I'd say, recharging its batteries. And you three? You all right?'

Annie and I nodded.

So did Claws.

'Frank, talk to the people in the launch. Tell them we have a passenger in labour.' He threw a number of switches, muttering to himself. 'Rudder locks. Control yoke locks. Mixture to Idle Cut Off.'

A passenger in labour?

What did the captain mean by that, exactly?

I had no idea.

The copilot unlocked the cockpit door.

A shrill cry of outrage resounded through the aircraft.

I knew what that cry portended. Poor Dr. B was being nibbled to death.

Annie and I had watched Ghost Ship. We had known from the beginning that Dr. B would suffer. I was sorry but I didn't think that her losing an ear or an eye really mattered that much. What truly mattered was that I had flown the plane and saved the day!

I was beside myself with excitement.

I was Biggles!

Mum and Dad would be thrilled.

I squeezed past Kelly, ran out of the flight deck, dashed past Dr. B's caged creatures and charged into our cabin, bursting with the most tremendous news.

'Mum! Dad! I flew the plane!' I cried triumphantly.

My announcement fell flat.

There was no reaction whatever, not so much as a 'Did you really, dear?'

Nobody paid me the slightest attention.

Being nine really sucks.

Nobody believes you.

Nobody listens to you.

I asked myself: What could possibly have happened here in this cabin that was more important than me flying a plane?

'Haven't had so much fun since I delivered a dugong,' said Dr. B, peeling off her gloves.

That was odd. Dr. B. was not missing any of her appendages. It had not been she who had cried out.

Who *had* cried out?

A dreadful suspicion began to dawn on me.

'Mum? Are you OK? You look floppy.'

Mum had deflated.

She had a silly smile on her face.

My heart sank.

For the first time in my life, my mother's smile was not for me.

Mum was smiling down at a small person she was holding in her arms, a small person wrapped in a blanket.

I was betrayed.

So was Annie.

Where were the flashing cameras and the reporters? Where were our medals? 'It was nothing,' I was ready to say. I was bursting to deny our heroism.

If only someone would ask! But nobody did.

I shivered. From this day on I would have to share my parents with a sister named Miranda. I could hear her peeing in her blanket. It was the waterfall of doom.

'Anthony, meet your brother.'

'My *what*?'

'Your brother! Come and say hello.'

I stared down at an angry little red face, all wrinkled and making a noise like a squirrel. 'Does it have a name?' I asked, seething.

'Charles.'

I had a *brother*.

A brother named after a Royal Baby.

My misery was complete.

VH-BRA Boeing PB2B-2R Catalina
Beachcomber
Barrier Reef Airways Scheduled service
Brisbane-Gladstone-Heron Island
(1947-1951)
Captain Stewart Middlemiss
Owner, Manager and Pilot
Pilot Frank Kelly
Assistant Manager and Pilot

The two pilots sat side by side in a wide cockpit with large windows all round. The aircraft had Pratt & Whitney twin Wasp engines cowled on the centre section with cooling gills, driving Hamilton variable-pitch propellers. There were seats for 22 passengers. Tropical salads were served.

Acknowledgement

I am most grateful to William G. Barry for looking over the manuscript of this book with the eye of an experienced pilot and for filling in the gaps in my understanding of what went on in the cockpit during my childhood adventure in 1951.

Postscript

My father was a true storyteller. My father's book 'Sponge, X and Y' was published by Penguin in 1979.

The editor, Kaye Webb, invited me to draw the illustrations and to design the cover for the book.

It was a joyful task to draw for Penguin my father's shining island with its nine palm trees, lodged on the back of a whale; and it was with fond memories of Heron Island that I added a white coral strand to set off my father's three fishes, Sponge, X and Y, and his hobgoblin with magic boots, and his nine monkeys.

A YOUNG
PUFFIN
ORIGINAL

Sponge, X and Y

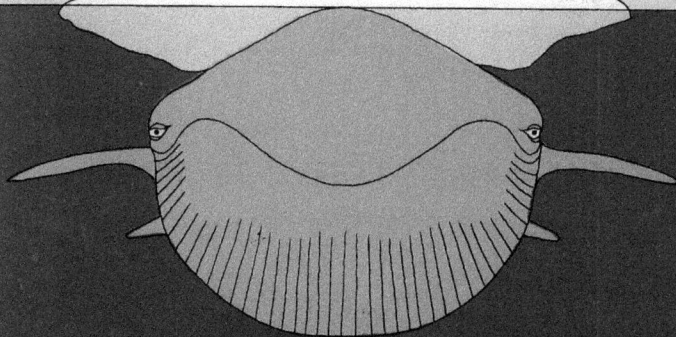

*A Tale of Three Fishy
Trouble-Shooters by*

HARRY BARTON

Sponge, X and Y, the three fishy trouble-shooters,
were ready to tackle any problem that came their
way. But they hardly expected two problems at once,
and a hobgoblin with magic boots . . .

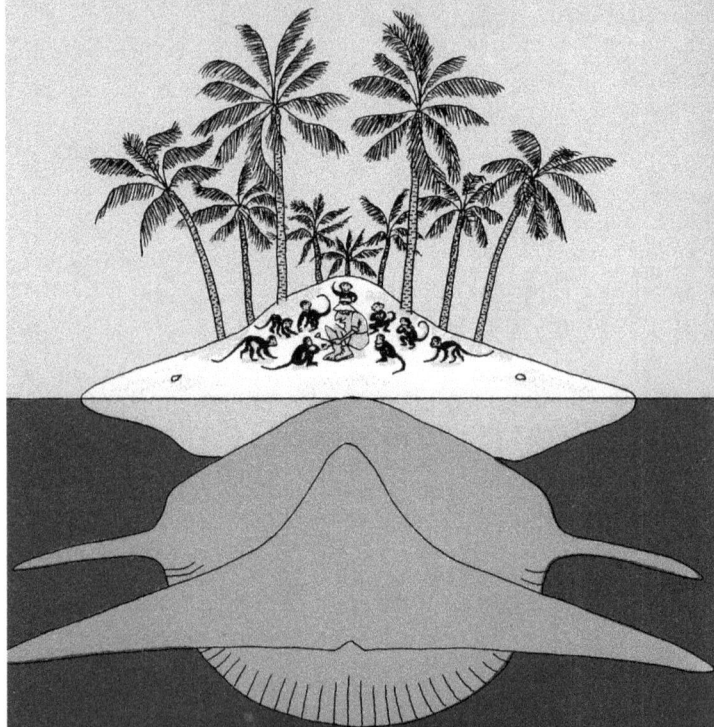

Cover and illustrations by Anthony Barton

United Kingdom 85p
Australia $2.50 (recommended)
Canada $2.50

ISBN 0 14
03.1124 6

BY THE SAME AUTHOR

The prequel to 'Claws in the Air'

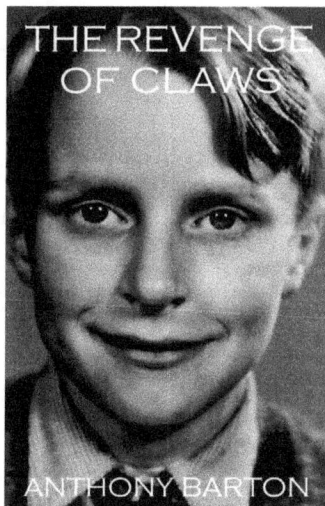

The ghost of a wronged cat stalks the decks of the RMS *Orcades* as she voyages from England to Australia. What will happens when the lights go out and the movie starts?

A fine evocation of childhood and an era. I remember the Orcades *from my youth.*

– Alan Cass

The various dimensions and arcs of Mr. Barton's plot click smoothly and satisfyingly into place. You are in very good hands on this ship. Relax and enjoy the voyage.

– David Stansfield, Sulby Hall

Available from Amazon.com

BY THE SAME AUTHOR

The Harriman Adventures

MIDSHIPMAN HARRIMAN

You can feel the wind in your face and
Napoleon breathing down your neck.
What if you are wounded in action and carried
below to the cockpit? What if somebody finds
out who you really are?

LIEUTENANT HARRIMAN

You can smell a storm coming. You don't think
any book could be this exciting? Just read a few
pages and then batten down the hatches.
You're in for the ride of your life.

CAPTAIN HARRIMAN

You can smell the stench of the prison island of
Cabrera. It is time to join the British fleet in an
all-out pitched battle to thwart Napoleon's
plan to assemble a Northern Confederacy.

All three Harriman books are available from Amazon.com

BY THE SAME AUTHOR

TERESA

You can hear the lions roaring and the hyenas laughing. You are in the wilds of Africa and your only hope of escaping the child soldiers lies in a raging river.
If only you could swim.

For other books and paintings please visit

THE AUTHOR'S WEBSITE

http://abart92.wix.com/author

oduct-compliance